Peachy
"The Warrior Princess"

Gabriela Duran

BALBOA
PRESS
A DIVISION OF HAY HOUSE

Copyright © 2014 Gabriela Duran.

All rights reserved. No part of this book may be used or reproduced by any means, graphic, electronic, or mechanical, including photocopying, recording, taping or by any information storage retrieval system without the written permission of the publisher except in the case of brief quotations embodied in critical articles and reviews.

Balboa Press books may be ordered through booksellers or by contacting:

Balboa Press
A Division of Hay House
1663 Liberty Drive
Bloomington, IN 47403
www.balboapress.com
1 (877) 407-4847

Because of the dynamic nature of the Internet, any web addresses or links contained in this book may have changed since publication and may no longer be valid. The views expressed in this work are solely those of the author and do not necessarily reflect the views of the publisher, and the publisher hereby disclaims any responsibility for them.

The author of this book does not dispense medical advice or prescribe the use of any technique as a form of treatment for physical, emotional, or medical problems without the advice of a physician, either directly or indirectly. The intent of the author is only to offer information of a general nature to help you in your quest for emotional and spiritual well-being. In the event you use any of the information in this book for yourself, which is your constitutional right, the author and the publisher assume no responsibility for your actions.

Any people depicted in stock imagery provided by Thinkstock are models, and such images are being used for illustrative purposes only.
Certain stock imagery © Thinkstock.

Printed in the United States of America.

ISBN: 978-1-4525-8693-9 (sc)
ISBN: 978-1-4525-8695-3 (hc)
ISBN: 978-1-4525-8694-6 (e)

Library of Congress Control Number: 2013921195

Balboa Press rev. date: 02/04/2014

Also by Gabriela Duran

"Desarrollo de una metodología de selección de alternativas de remediación para suelos impactados por pesticidas, con base en índices de coeficiencia". México, December 2003.

Contents

Dedication xi
Foreword xiii
Preface xix
Acknowledgement xxiii

PART I 1
    Introduction 3
    Conclusion 27
    Some resources on finding a pet are 31

PART II - For teens, young adults and adults 33
    Learning about animal communicators and to
        open my mind 40
    Meet the pack 48
        Andrew 48
        Fergie 53
        Peachy 62
        Tyra 65
    Diet 68
    Zoos and Circuses 73
    Pet stores 74
    Finding a good breeder 78
    Finding a trainer 85
    Veterinarians 90
    How can you help? 92
    Adults, seniors and special dogs 95

PART III - Sharing our family Pictures 99
    Introduction 101
    Fergie May 2006 102
    May 2006 Fergie and Andrew playing 103

July 20, 2006 Fergie in the new basement couch 104
Andrew in our bed fall of 2006 105
Winter 2006 Fergie and mom 106
Ricardo and Fergie winter 2006 107
Fergie and Andrew in bed 109
Andrew waiting for his ball 110
How I met Peachy 111
The adoption process 112
Peachy on the way home 114
Peachy's first bed 116
Peachy first trip 117
Peachy's first home haircut 118
Peachy's first blanket experience 119
Peachy's first sweater 120
Peachy first belly rub 121
Peachy October 2007 122
November 2007 123
Peachy being more herself 124
Her first public appearance 125
October 5th, 2008 126
Peachy's profile 127
Becoming a Therapy Dog 129
Peachy summer 2009 131
Summer 2009 132
April 2010, Fergie's Birthday 133
December 2009 134
Peachy and me 135
Fergie and Peachy 2009 136
Peachy Begging for the first time on her hind legs 138
At the retirement home with Daddy 139
Peachy first Valentine's day 140
Peachy's first Halloween picture 141
Peachy's first Christmas 142
Christmas 2008 144

A new bed 145
In the TV room September 2011 147
April 29, 2012 149
October 28, 2012 150
Toronto, November 15th, 2011 152
September 1st 2012, Birch run 153
Peachy at the Back yard door 155
Peachy in Ricardo's arms 156
Yogurt face 158
April 2012 159
Peachy's last picture with Santa 161
Peachy in Veracruz 162
December 23, 2012 164
At grandma's snoozing with my Sissy 166
At grandma's Begging 168
At grandmas trying my new snow suit 171
Coming back from Mexico, In Houston airport
    tram January 2013 172
Sleeping at Mariana's January 2013 173
At my old house January 2013 174
At the residence inn 175
Cuddling with my dada 177
May 15th 2013 my Birthday celebration at Residence Inn ... 179
At the dog park June 2013 180
At laser acupuncture therapy for my legs 181
August 17th, 2013: first night at the new house 182
August 28th, 2013 183
Feeding time! September 2013 185
September 24th, 2013 186
The practice tent 189
September 26th, 2013 190
Peachy's last bed 192
September 27th, 2013 193
After Peachy 198

Peachy's leg 199
My letters to Peachy 205
Ricardo's Facebook Memorial 210
Gaby's Facebook Memorial 212
October 5th 2013 213
Peachy's Gift 217

National Mill dog Rescue 225
Afterword 229
Abbreviations 233
Glossary 235
About the Author 237

Dedication

To all the puppy mill dogs in the world, honoring the ones that never make it out to enjoy life as a family pet and those that are still suffering the horrors of it.

This is also for the dogs like Peachy who have made it out and are now living happily in new homes and for those dogs that are in a rescue organization while awaiting their forever-family.

To Peachy, without her this story would have never been written. We love you little girl.

To Ricardo, who never imagine he was marrying the crazy dog lady I am, who has always been supportive, whose life was also changed by Peachy.

To my soul family, my spiritual teachers and my soul sisters, thank you for all your love and support and for believing in me. Love you all.

To Pinto, who after 14 years of unconditional love was too tired to keep going, his legs were starting to fail; he was old, wise and sick. He left us on December 20th, 2013. Thank you Pinto boy for all your teachings, for being part of the pack that awakened me. We miss you deeply and remember you with deep love and gratitude. We know you are in a better place.

To all kids and adults, please believe you can be the change that you want to see in this world. Never stop dreaming, never stop achieving and fulfilling your dreams.

A good percentage of the profits of this book will go to help stop puppy-mills, because we believe no dog soul should live the horror of a puppy-mill.

Foreword

Peachy is indeed a Warrior Princess.

We met under somewhat remarkable circumstances, as we don't live close or even in the same country. I first "met" her when her human mom, Gaby called me. Concerned for Peachy's life and her unnecessary suffering, she desperately wanted to know what her dog's wishes were. The vets were pretty certain the tiny poodle wouldn't make it.

While it may sound far-fetched to some, we all have the innate ability to know so much more than what our rational mind and five senses tell us. Everything is energy and has a specific vibrational frequency, even thoughts and emotions. As an animal communicator, or intuitive, even long distance I am able to get a "sense" for what an animal would like, how they feel in their bodies, what they are thinking and sensing, and even if they feel it is their "time" to take that final breath into spirit.

It clearly was not Peachy's time. She had more life to live, and more love to give. And especially more treats to eat! To everyone's surprise she came home from the veterinary hospital that first time.

Anyone who has ever lost an animal dear to them, ever rescued a terrified neglected animal, ever felt guilty like they should have done more, ever wondered who these animal angels were, ever needed hope in the darkest of nights, then this story is for you.

Peachy's rags to riches life chronicled here will undoubtedly bring you from tears to victory laps and back again. But the real behind-the-scenes story is one of human evolution, not animal.

The one that the author plays out for many of us with her raw courage in sharing her journey in such an authentic and soul-searching way. She is not preaching here, but exposing her often trial and error discoveries, as they unfold. She is willing to look at all parts of her journey in the light of growing from her experiences;

and challenging her own views and judgments of what seems "right" and best.

This is real courage. The courage to continue to question and go deeper within, to trust our own feelings and inner knowing over what is culturally accepted, to change when we discover that what we were taught does not feel like our truth anymore, and ultimately to open your heart to loving again when you know it will be broken over and over.

For the life of a puppy mill dog may be one of the most heart-wrenching "tales." When these playful, curious and generally good natured animals have truly lost their trust in humanity, it speaks volumes.

I have worked with hundreds of rescue and feral animals, yet the puppy mill dogs I have worked with were the most tortured and terrified souls I ever met. They knew first hand some of the most callous, non-caring, and downright cruel humans imaginable. Their physical restrictions of never being allowed out of a small crate can create some serious deformities and some of the most bizarre health and fear-based behavior problems imaginable.

I worked with a small mixed breed dog in a shelter who had an odd fear-based behavior that was mis-labeled with seizures as she collapsed, splaying her back legs on the pavement when walked, as she was terrified of concrete. Another terrier had so much fear aggression after 7 years in a cage, he bit everyone who came near him and several vets said he was too dangerous and should be euthanized. I was able to help both of them release their understandable rage, fear and deep mistrust. A week later they were successfully adopted, against all odds.

The amazing thing about dogs (and most animals actually) is their ability to let go of the past and love again. Like Peachy, it may take a while if they have been treated in a pattern of neglect and abuse for long periods. But many of them have shown remarkable ability to reform their well-deserved mistrust, hopelessness, fear and even aggression, which can only be seen as a spiritual trait of forgiveness, for it sure doesn't seem like humanity deserves another chance sometimes.

Another puppy mill terrier I met had an added trauma; she was caught in the Katrina hurricane and ended up on the streets, completely feral. She was so afraid she quaked when anyone was around, and while she had started to improve and connect better, as it happened she broke free on a walk –with me!--and after days of searching, was hit by a car. Though I felt deeply responsible, I had a most amazing "visit" with what I can only describe as her angelic spirit. Her inspiring message is a teaching that has never left me:

> *"I am an angel of Light.*
> *You recognized my intelligence, my sensitivity, my purity*
> *For that I am ever grateful*
> *It has truly freed me from the bondage of the body.*
> *I don't know how to thank you all for helping me to complete my mission--my journey*
> *To Heal, despite trauma.*
> *To Love, despite pain.*
> *To Forgive, despite blame.*
> *I became Whole when you loved me. When you saw me.*
> *Not broken and scared—but sensitive and wise.*
> *You reminded me who I was. What I could be.*
> *It freed me from the karma of the flesh—I could return to Spirit—mission accomplished. I want everyone to understand what you understood when I presented my true self. That all is in Divine Order. That beings are not limited to the form they choose. That comings and goings are much easier, and much more complex, than you imagine.*
> *It is all laid out ahead. Events, timing, even difficulties. We choose our difficulties with great care, for the gems they hold within. In Spirit we celebrate the difficulties equally with the victories. There is no difference—for they all bring us to the Knowing, to the Oneness.*

My journey has touched many people, you don't even know how many. This is the REAL story. Not a missing dog, not a dog hit by a car, not a leash that slipped, not even a "Katrina" puppy mill victim. These are all incidentals to the divine mission I took on, and by the way, accomplished. I had to bring people together, in small ways, and in big ways. People you don't even know, drove around, put up flyers, prayed, connected in their concern. Others saw me as a survivor, not a victim, not starving, running fast and strong. You see, perceptions changed. In small ways, and in big ways.

You saw my true self, and as a result I was able to remove sadness and pain from your "loss", lessen your guilt and feelings of over-responsibility for things well beyond your—or any human's—control. For this you will be forever changed—forever grateful—and much more capable of doing the work you were sent to do. Without the burden of misunderstanding life and death, and your role in preserving neither, but merely and heroically I might add, seeing things as they truly ARE, seeing TRUTH and sharing this so others (human and animal) may understand their true nature, their divinity, their special mission here on this planet.

And that is Enough. Enough for any life. I had enough –Life. I had enough—Time. Enough—Love. In one drop of human tears, enough Caring. And enough—Sadness. It is not time for sadness. It is time for celebration. I return Home—joyfully and with great pride. Mission accomplished. More than was speculated. I am very pleased. From my vantage point, this life was a great success. I know this is hard for you to grasp, especially right now as you grieve the loss of the One you knew. But I am not that one only—four legs, soft fur, sad eyes. And I am not even the story—Katrina victim, puppy mill, runaway, etc.

I am the Light of God shimmering in Divine Dogness one moment, and in a flash,

I am Sunlight
I am golden rain pouring down
to soothe the hot brow of Mother Earth,
I am a dancing star.
I am... You."

Just as Peachy and Gaby chose, I encourage you to take positive loving action rather than get angry. For anger is the very energy that creates the realities of puppy mills and mistreatment of any life to begin with. Use the anger and pain you do feel when innocents are hurt, for the fuel to make a difference, to speak up, to forgive--first yourself and then all of us--for harboring fear, greed and unconscious behaviors of all kinds. The animals can show you how.

This book is not a rant against injustice, nor is it merely another love story between human and canine. It is universal and practical simultaneously. The author shares simple ways everyone can make a difference, both in your pets' life, and in your communities.

The funny thing is, we often think we are rescuing someone, only to find out *we* were the ones who needed rescuing. One puppy at a time. One belief at a time. One heart and soul at a time.

Peachy's difficult life was not in vain. Quite the contrary, she taught us all what courage is, and what value there is in living, even when there are seemingly insurmountable challenges. Uncomplaining, forgiving, overcoming fears great and small, and never turning to anger, Peachy never closed her heart.

Xena, move over. There is a new model for us, a softer strength, a quieter courage. When I think Warrior Princess, I think of Peachy.

With great respect and love,
Kumari
Intuitive Healer and Animal Mystic
www.KumariHealing.com

Preface

In the summer of 2007 I finally fulfilled my dream of having a toy poodle. I decided this dog needed to be an adopted one because for many years, I had rescued dogs in my home country, as well as I had volunteered for different rescue organization, so it was time for me to put my money where my mouth is.

In my early days as a dog rescuer, I knew I had to put together a book for kids, so I could start touching the hearts of younger generations, and in doing so making them become part of the solution, not part of the problem.

This idea came to me in 2003 while I was studying away from home, doing my master's degree and dedicating all my spare time to rescuing dogs and volunteering for a rescue organization. volunteering for a rescue organization was my childhood dream, but since I was raised in a small town where there was not such a thing, when I moved to Monterrey, I learned there were several rescue organizations I could volunteer for, that's exactly what I did with my spare time. I did not have tons of spare time since I was studying at a very demanding University, working for the University as a research assistant, writing a thesis and dating but because being among the people of this rescue group and among dogs made my heart sing, I made the time. I really felt at my happiest while working as a volunteer for the dogs.

As a volunteer, I used to help picking up dogs from the streets whether the dogs were healthy or injured, driving the dogs to their Vet appointments, selling tickets for different fund raising activities, hanging posters at my University, spending my weekends either at the shelter helping keep the dogs clean or at the adoption fairs we had at the malls and expos, and last but not least working in the kids campaigns.

The rescue foundation I was part of had a shelter; we used to work with kids from orphanages and schools with a program one of the volunteers developed. This program was all about teaching kids animals have feelings and they only want to be loved and accepted by humans so that's why it was wrong to be mean and abusive to animal whether they were yours or strays, or to abandon them.

The program also had the "no bite program" where we used to take one of the rescue dogs to an elementary school and teach the kids how to approach a dog. Kids loved dogs and for them to have a dog visiting was amazing. That also gave us the opportunity to tell the story of the dog to the kids. This organization was one of the best organized groups and we were able to do a lot for homeless dogs in Mexico.

I got side tracked as I was too young and that same year I graduated, so it was time for me to find a job. I was under a lot of pressure trying to find a job. I finally found a job in my home town so I moved back home and after I started working, I kept rescuing dogs from the streets, I knew I needed to do more but my personal issues caught up with me, also my parents were not supportive of my rescues, so I was not allowed to bring any dog home, all this made me forget about writing the book.

To make matters worse I used to drive one hour from home to the industrial plant I worked at. Every day on the highway, I saw dogs hit by cars, starving, dying or dead on the road, it was like my morning torture, like God was trying to send me a message, to focus on what was important, but at that point working, making money and earning my freedom from my parents was my number one priority so I learned to do what I could for the dogs and kept shoving down my feelings in order to keep going.

After all in my home town I did not have the support system of the whole rescue organization and my hundreds of friends that were volunteers there, but I did find a way to enroll my two friend who are veterinarians into helping me with my rescues.

In 2006 I married and moved to Canada, I also started paying attention to my repressed feelings. It was like an avalanche had caught me. In 2007 I was fortunate enough to be able to adopt

Peachy. Peachy was a puppy mill mama and even though I had been rescuing dogs from the streets of Mexico pretty much my entire life, and I had witnessed animal abuse and neglect to the worse, I honestly thought I had seen it all in Mexico but I had never encounter a dog that had as many issues as Peachy had.

I went into research to learn what was this puppy mill all about, after all I had never heard of something like that before. To this day I don't think something like that exists in Mexico. In Mexico there is still a lot of back yard breeders and people that just don't fix their animals, so a lot of "ups" litters, as well as tons of strays, unwanted pets and still many breeders. But so far I don't know of any puppy mills there.

So for me was shocking, this was something new, something disturbing to my soul (really I'm very strong and don't get disturbed easily, especially when it comes to animal abuse because I have seen a lot), but this puppy mill images and papers I was reading where getting me enraged, making me feel I needed to stop it. I could not believe this little five pound fluffy poodle had survived living at the puppy mill for five years. No wonder when she made it to rescue she did not want to go anywhere else.

I knew I needed to tell her story, but again I got side tracked by working on my own childhood issues and doing my best to keep this little girl happy and healthy. So not until summer 2012, I started writing and then finally this year I decided to publish.

I hope you enjoy the story, is a story of love, life, and personal growth, from my heart to yours.

Acknowledgement

Special Thanks.

I want to thank four amazing women who supported and helped me make this book possible.

Kumari; from Kumarihealing.com; who is my dog's animal communicator and a wonderful healer. I also appreciate her help in connecting me with Linda. Kumari saw how important it is to me to help dogs and to accomplish my dream of publishing this story.

Linda, who with her experience guided me through the whole publishing process, she always encouraged me to keep moving forward and she believed in my writing skills. She has become a good friend.

Gabriela Benitez, my illustrator. She is someone I have known for several years. I knew she was a teacher but yet it never occurred to me she has a bachelor in arts and as an artist she specializes in animal portraits. Without her work this story would never have come to life. She came to me at the right time and for that I'm grateful.

And last but not least, I give thanks to Aly from Illinois Cocker Rescue who believed in me, trusted me with Peachy's life. Even though she hadn't previously done adoptions out of state. In doing so she help me embark on a journey of healing and learning from Peachy's very old soul and wisdom. Without her, Peachy would have not had a second chance after being released from the puppy mill. Without Aly's trust in me, Peachy probably would have spent many more years at the rescue farm curled up like a football instead of enjoying life as a spoiled princess dog and learning how to be a dog from her sister Fergie. Peachy wouldn't have been able to bring happiness to the seniors she used to visit as a Therapy dog. And just as important, Peachy wouldn't have been able to touch the hearts of millions of kids and families with her story.

Without this group of women who came to me at the right time and without the superior force that put them on my path, this dream of telling this story and in doing so changing lives would never have come to pass. I'm extremely blessed and grateful for finally being able to educate other generations and save more dogs.

Thanks with all our heart.
Gabriela, Fergie and Peachy.

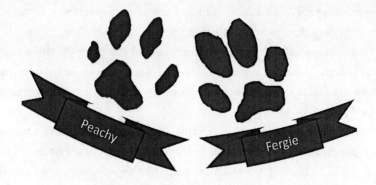

Part I

Introduction

When I asked God to send somebody to help stop puppy-mills, I realized I'm somebody.

My intention is to touch the lives of every kid in the world and their families and in doing so change the life of millions of abandoned and unwanted pets, especially the ones that are waiting day after day in the puppy-mills for their torture to end, and all those puppies waiting at pet stores to be sold to a good family that will keep them forever. Promoting adoption, spaying and neutering, ending puppy-mills, backyard breeding, and dogs being sold in pet stores is my first goal in publishing this book.

I also would like to improve the lives of many family pets that are being neglected. If you own a pet, be committed to make it part of your day-to-day activities and treat it as you treat your children. After all, dogs are like little kids--innocent. They just want to be loved and approved by their human.

With all my heart I share the story of the rescue that has impacted my life the most. This is the story of Peachy, a little apricot poodle, who was so neglected and abused that no one wanted her. I hope her story inspires you to change the life of a living soul. It doesn't have to be a dog; it could be any animal or another human being. After all, we are all souls having an earth experience as some recognized authors said.

Gabriela Duran

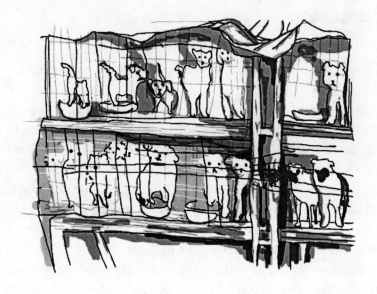

Peachy is such a tiny girl. Some bad people decided she would be a good addition to their commercial breeding facility. In the place where they breed dogs, they keep her in a small crate and make sure she will have babies every six months.

Peachy was probably born in a puppy-mill herself, and her fate was to become a puppy-mill mama. She never lost faith in a brighter better future, even though all the years of bad experiences she had as a breeding dog in the puppy-mill.

Every day in her crate is a bad experience. There is not enough food and the crate is never clean. She dreams of having a chance to get out of the crate and run around in the green grass of the beautiful acreage that surround the puppy-mill.

She can't understand why?; If there is so much green space and land at the puppy mill, why does she have to be in a crate all the time?. This makes her very sad.

Gabriela Duran

Summers are the toughest time. The crates are stacked one on top of the other and there isn't any fresh air. She often gets poo or pee on top of her from the dog in the crate above her.

Winters are not easy either, because there is no heat and she gets cold. The place where she lives has cold, cold winters. Peachy wishes she had a nice warm blanket and a soft bed.

Bath time isn't fun. Because there are so many dogs, sometimes they just get hosed down with cold water. They are left all wet, and have to wait until they dry off on their own. Peachy wishes she could dry off fast and not feel so miserable. Peachy hopes to never feel this way again!

Peachy "The Warrior Princess"

Peachy grows and her crate feels even smaller. She has to spread her toes out and stand on the wires of the bottom of the crate. Her body is forced to be in awkward positions, so she can fit in the crate, her legs and feet start to get malformed. Peachy doesn't understand why this is happening to her body. She is sad, but every time she falls asleep, she dreams of better times coming her way.

When Peachy is six-months old, she is forced to reproduce and she has her first set of puppies.

Peachy loves her puppies. She is a good, loving mama to them. That's why she can't understand when the puppy-mill owner takes her babies away to sell them to a pet store. Peachy is terrified and sad because she can't stop the owner from taking her puppies away. She tries to explain that her babies are too young to live without her. She cries and barks, trying to say that she would rather have her babies meet loving families that will take care of them for a lifetime. She is doing her best to get the puppy mill owner to stop, and let her keep her babies. But nothing stops the puppy-mill owner. He sells the puppies to the pet store.

Peachy gets really sad, and she wonders where her babies are now, she spends her days laying in her crate, dreaming of her babies and hoping they are alive and well taken care off.

The babies are sad because they miss Peachy and they cry every day and night, hoping someone will give them the same love, care and attention that Peachy used to give them. They can't understand why Peachy is not with them? Why strangers are handling them? Why their new "house" is a clear box where everybody can see them.

There is too much light in the new place, too many people, this place is nothing like the puppy mill and yet Peachy is not with them. What they don't understand is why they are at a pet store now.

The babies see Peachy in their dreams and that helps them fall asleep night after night in the pet store glass box.

The puppy-mill owner decides it is shower day for all the dogs, but this time he doesn't want to hose them down, he has time, so he takes them one by one and sinks them in a bucket of water. The dogs are terrified and the ones that refuse are forced into the bucket while the rest of the dogs watch from inside their crates.

Peachy saw what happened to some of the other dogs during bathing time, so she decides to behave because she knows there are better times ahead. She sits and lets the puppy mill owner bathe her. She puts up with the rough scrubbing and the cold water. She tries to think about her dream for better times, in her dreams she still thinks of her babies all the time, she hopes they are happy and safe.

After another six months have passed, it is time for Peachy to have babies again. Peachy is happy and hopes this time she gets to keep her puppies a little longer, so she is on her best behavior. She cleans the crate after her puppies and does everything she can think of to try to convince the puppy-mill owner to let her keep the puppies.

But the evil owner comes with the pet shop owner again. Peachy knows they are there to get her puppies and she barks and cries but nothing stops the evil owner from taking the puppies. Because her barking started a whole barking revolution at the puppy-mill, the evil owner decides to punish her by making her go without food and water for several days. He believes this will teach her a lesson. Peachy goes through the punishment, she feels very sad and weak but she is very smart and learns the lesson, she also learns that things may not change soon. She asks the stars to take care of her puppies and to send loving families to them, families that will give her little fur angels all their love. She hopes the families will love her puppies as much as she does. She prays for them to find homes soon so they don't have to spend a long time in the pet store.

Peachy is a smart girl and she decides she is going to be submissive from now on. Maybe, she thinks, this will convince the evil owner to treat her better. She cleans her crate, sleeps most of the time, never barks, never complains about showers, and she keeps producing healthy puppies every six months. Even when the evil owner comes to take the puppies, as sad and frustrated as she is, she just kisses her puppies' goodbye and sends her wishes to the stars that her puppies will find loving homes. She knows her puppies are afraid, but she keeps them as calm as she can. She knows her puppies are way too young and need her to survive, but she also knows there is nothing she can do, but pray for the babies to survive and find loving families.

The evil owner and the pet store owner can almost see how Peachy is grateful that her puppies are going on a quest to find good homes. Can it be possible that, they see she is grateful that her babies don't have to live the horror she lives day after day?

Three years pass and Peachy is still on her best behavior. Six groups of her puppies have been taken away, but she is still in her small wire crate, she has been to auctions and she keeps being treated poorly. She has not been able to convince the evil owner to let her and the other dogs run around on the property, no one is allowed to get out of their crates. She still has top neighbors that keep sending their waste down to her. The place smells horrible, no matter what she does to keep it clean. She is a little sad but she is confident better times will come.

She keeps sending her wishes of a better life for herself and all the dogs in the puppy-mill to the stars night after night. She also gives thanks that her babies are living in loving homes with wonderful families, even though they were born at the puppy-mill with no comfort at all and then taken away from their mom at a young age to be sold in a pet store. She doesn't know if her puppies are ok for sure but she doesn't loose her faith.

Another year passes and Peachy is starting to have trouble producing puppies for the evil owner. She doesn't know what is going on, but this year she was only able to produce one puppy. She hugs her little girl and explains to her that soon a man will come with the evil owner and he will take her away. Peachy says, "That doesn't mean I don't love you, it is just the way things happen around here. I'll always love you and be here for you, as I have been here for all your brothers and sisters." Peachy also said, "Don't be afraid. Don't be lonely. You only need to look up at the stars to know I'm sending you all my love every night." Peachy and her baby fall asleep hugging each other.

Gabriela Duran

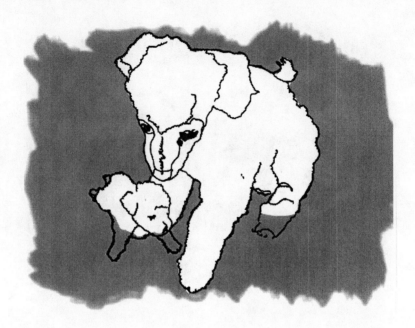

Sure enough, a week later the evil owner comes in to the puppy-mill with the pet store owner and they take Peachy's last baby. Peachy is worried because she doesn't know what is going to happen to her now that she can't have any more babies. Usually the dogs that are not able to produce puppies disappear. She is also aware that her body is starting to show the sign of malnourishment, her legs look twisted now and she is not looking as pretty as she did in earlier years.

She falls asleep thinking that something better is coming her way and maybe the other dogs that were not productive have been taken into the evil owner house. After all, none of her peers from the mill have been in the evil owner house, so nobody knows for sure where the nonproductive dogs have gone. Peachy has hope and faith, and that is what has been keeping her alive all these years. She decides she is not giving up. She keeps looking at the stars and sending them her wishes for a better life, not only for her, but for the other dogs too. She also asks the stars, as she always does, to take care of her babies wherever they may be.

Meanwhile, the evil owner is thinking how he is going to get rid of Peachy and a few other girls that have not had puppies lately. The evil owner thinks of all the cruel ways he has used to dispose of dogs in the past, but this is starting to take a toll on him. He finds himself waking up in the middle of the night with nightmares about the horrible things he has done to innocent dogs, he thinks of ways to auction these dogs, perhaps have a puppy-mill auction, so he doesn't have to kill them himself and he can make some money out of these beaten souls. He thinks that if he can sell the dogs as productive dogs, another puppy miller will end up with the problem and will have to dispose of them. Suddenly, he gets the idea of calling a rescue organization and he follows through it.

The evil owner gets on the phone and calls a rescue in the area run by a lady named Angel. Angel answers the phone and the man tells her he has a few dogs he needs to get rid of because he has a puppy-mill and he has some dogs that are no longer productive. They are mainly females, he says, and some are still pretty young. He tells Angel he will happily give them away to Angel's rescue with the condition that Angel has to keep his contact information a secret and not tell anyone where his facility is located. Angel agrees and gets his address.

Angel gets off the phone and rushes to get kennels in her van. She has horrible feelings towards the man, but she decides she is going to focus on his good actions and the fact that he no longer wants to use cruel ways to dispose of his nonproductive dogs. So with her emotions in check and her van loaded with empty kennels, she gets in the van and drives as fast as she can to get the dogs. All she could think of is that finally she was contacted by the puppy-mill owner and now she is going to be able to help all these innocent dogs.

Meanwhile, Peachy is really worried. After all, a month has passed since the evil owner sold her last baby and he has not yet come back for her. What Peachy doesn't know, however, is that all those years of prayers, good behavior, positive thinking, wishing upon stars, hope and faith, are about to pay off because someone has been keeping an eye on her from heaven and has decided to make her dream come true and answer all her prayers."

Angel finally arrives at the puppy-mill facility. She is nervous because she doesn't know what to expect from this man. All she has heard from her fellow rescuers is that this man runs the worse puppy-mill in history and that he is evil and keeps the dogs in horrible conditions, sometimes even letting the dogs die of thirst or hunger. Angel gets out of the van to meet with the monster. She knocks at his door with a smile. After all, she wants to be able to keep helping all the retired dogs this guy may have in the future, so she puts her best face on and behaves as nice and kind as she can be. She keeps reminding herself, "You are here for the dogs, so be calm, patient, and don't show your real feelings towards this guy."

The evil owner answers the door and immediately starts giving Angel the dogs one by one, without even saying hello to her. All Angel sees are filthy dogs in need of immediate baths and hugs. The dogs are fearful, but something inside them seems to give them hope. Angel starts loading the dogs in the empty kennels she has in her van. The dogs are shih Tzu's, poodles, cocker spaniels, Maltese, yorkies, Pomeranians, yorkie mixes, and cocker mixes. She feels angry and sad for the dogs but she knows if she shows any emotion the evil owner will never give her dogs again and he will probably stop passing the dogs to her. She just keeps smiling and nodding at him while he tells her how bad these dogs are.

Angel's van is now full and there is one more dog to go. This dog is a tiny little apricot toy poodle that is all curled up like a football. Angel immediately notices this dog has an ear problem and even though her van is full she will not leave her behind. This tiny girl is Peachy, the last one to get out of the puppy-mill, and the one that needs the most medical attention, love and hugs.

Angel gets Peachy in her hands and asks the evil owner if he will be so kind to let her know the date of birth of all the dogs she is taking. The evil owner says he doesn't have accurate information, but he knows Peachy was born on May 15, 2000 because he bought her at a puppy-mill auction. Angel thanks the evil owner and gets in her van with a shaky Peachy in her arms.

Angel drives to the vet's office with a very fearful and stinky tiny poodle in her lap. The little poodle is all curled up and shaking. Angel decides to give her a name, because at the puppy-mill none of the dogs have names. They all have livestock tags pierced on their right ear with a number, so she calls this girl Peachy. She tells her, "Peachy don't worry, I promise you are safe now. My name is Angel and I will find you a forever home."

At the vet's office all the dogs are shaved down, shampooed, and then they get medical checkups to make sure they don't have any contagious illnesses. After all, Angel has more dogs at the rescue ranch that she has already nurtured back to health and she needs to keep those dogs healthy. At the vet's office the staff knows Angel well. Because everyone admires her and her work, they help Angel with special pricing for all her rescue dogs.

Peachy gets medical attention for the first time in her life. The vet tells Angel, "Peachy's left ear has been severely damaged and it will need to be reconstructed with surgery. Her ear probably was caught on the crate's door at the puppy-mill because it doesn't look like Peachy has been in a dog fight." Peachy is malnourished, too, and her teeth are all rotten so they may need to be pulled to prevent infection and to prevent infection travelling to other parts of her body like her heart and blood stream.

Angel decides Peachy should be the first dog to have surgery. She will get spayed and while she is under the anesthetic they will fix her left ear and her teeth. Peachy has other signs of the puppy-mill: her paws have expanded from standing for five years in a wire crate and her front legs are a little curved, so when Peachy stands she looks like a little bulldog. But she is so tiny and has such a unique peach color that Angel believes Peachy is going to go to a forever home in no time. After all, people come to her rescue ranch looking for tiny unique dogs every day and Peachy fits this description.

The rest of the dogs also get the medical attention they need. They all get spayed and neutered and their teeth are cleaned so they look their best for possible adoptions.

After a couple of days at the vet clinic, Angel finally gets to pick up all the dogs to take them to her rescue ranch. Angel's ranch is located on twenty acres of fenced grass. Her home is there, too, so the dogs she gets from the puppy-mills get the chance to run around the house and also learn the skills they need for family life, such as eating real food, doing their business out in the grass, playing with toys, playing with other dogs, and interacting with humans. After all, these dogs have lived in tiny crates for years and they need to transition to freedom and family life.

When Angel arrives home, the first thing she does after making sure the fence is locked is to take the kennels from her van. She opens the kennel doors and lets the dogs get out on their own and run around the property. To her surprise, little Peachy is still curled up inside the kennel that transported her from the vet clinic to the rescue ranch. She thinks Peachy will recover in a couple days, so she helps Peachy out of her kennel. Peachy doesn't know what to do when she stands in the grass. She keeps looking at Angel with her big sad eyes and trying to hide back in the kennel.

Angel is an experienced rescuer, so she keeps introducing the new dogs to the other dogs at the rescue ranch. She is patient too, with their new diet, because she knows from personal experience that a natural diet will make these dogs stronger sooner. She feeds them raw food that she personally prepares for them.

Angel works with Peachy every day to help her overcome her fear of humans, her fear to be out in an open space. She encourages Peachy to be part of the group activities like ball playing, tug of war, and chasing each other, but Peachy's years at the mill and the memories of all her puppies being taken away from her have taken a toll. Peachy, despite all of Angel's efforts, shuts down and curls up every time a human gets close to her. Peachy only trusts Angel, and is comfortable only with her. That makes her adoption into a good family a little challenging. Peachy is the kind of dog most people want to adopt, but she keeps shutting down and ruining her adoption interviews.

Peachy's fears and memories have made tons of possible adopters walk away from her, thinking it will be too difficult to work with her. Angel has started to think Peachy will live at the rescue until the day she goes to heaven, but remember—someone is looking over Peachy's shoulder and has the power to make Peachy's dream come true. Angel decides to advertise Peachy as well as all her other dogs through adoption websites to increase their possibilities of being adopted into loving homes. This will give Angel the opportunity to rescue, rehabilitate and rehome more dogs, too.

An unusual person has decided that for her birthday, despite having two other dogs, she wants to adopt a toy poodle in need. She has convinced her husband that they will do this. She is very persuasive, for she has made it her mission in life to help animals. Ever since their move to Canada, she has been looking into adopting a dog, but it has to be a special dog. Where she and her husband live in Canada, stray dogs are not as common as in her native country, where every day she saw stray dogs on the streets in need of help. This woman's name is Gaby, and she found a couple of poodles in need on the internet. So she started sending emails and making phone calls.

Her husband, Ricardo, is still iffy about getting another dog. After all, they moved Gaby's two senior dogs from their home country to Canada. If they move back, or move to the United States they will then have three dogs to move. If they stay in Canada, all the dog services are more expensive than in their country. But despite his efforts to sway her thinking, Gaby convinces Ricardo that all she wants for her birthday is to adopt a dog in need and save a life.

Gaby gets in touch with Angel and discovers Angel's rescue is in the USA, at a place that is nine-and-a-half hours away from where Gaby lives. Angel tells Gaby up front that despite having passed the adoption requirements and the phone interview, Gaby has to keep in mind that something may go wrong during the in-person interview and Gaby may end up making the trip with the whole family, dogs included, for nothing. Gaby agrees, because she has rescued and re-homed dogs before and she understands where Angel is coming from. Angel also tells Gaby to be prepared to come back home without a dog because she only gives dogs up for adoption in areas where her rescue is located so she can keep an eye on the adoptive parents. Angel says she is making an exception because it seems to be a good home for Peachy. Peachy has been with Angel for two years now, and Angel's main priority is to make sure Peachy is happy. Gaby agrees to all the conditions Angel sets.

Gaby talks to Ricardo. He thinks it is crazy to drive 9.5 hours to possibly come back empty-handed. But he has promised Gaby she can adopt a dog for her birthday, so to keep his promise, off they go. They load their SUV with their other dogs and then drive all the way to the rescue ranch. The trip was done on a long weekend, because Ricardo figured that will give them more time to travel all the way back and from northern Ontario to Illinois State. They started traveling on a Friday evening after Ricardo finished work; they drove three quarters of way and stayed in a pet friendly hotel, doing the rest of the trip early Saturday morning making sure they will be on time for their interview at the rescue ranch.

When they arrived in the little town where the rescue is located and start to get ready for the exiting day ahead, Gaby could feel her adrenaline building up. This was her first experience as an adoptive parent in an American rescue. She has always been on the other side, as the one who was interviewing people and giving her rescue dogs to good homes. Finally Gaby and Ricardo are on their way, driving to the rescue ranch, following all the instructions Angel had given: where to park; how to wait so they don't disturb the resident dogs; if the dogs are outside, wait until she has control of them before opening the gate and entering the place; and so on. Gaby and Ricardo get their dogs Fergie and Andrew out of the SUV and enter the ranch. Gaby is wearing a poodle T-shirt and the first thing Angel says is, "I notice your shirt. It's nice but please keep in mind you may go back without a dog." Gaby just nods, because something inside her says she is going to go home with Peachy in her arms, and she's filled up with emotion that had her throat closed, she knew she would cry if she tried to talk.

After chatting for a few minutes and giving Gaby and Ricardo instructions, Angel goes in the house and then brings a couple of poodles out. These dogs are already over their fear of people and one special black female, with the Spanish name Karina, immediately bonds with Gaby's two poodles, Andrew and Fergie. Peachy is in Angel's arms, curled in her favorite position, a football shape, and she is shaking. Gaby can't wait to get Peachy in her arms, but Angel reminds her, "Peachy has been like this since we got her. She doesn't even know how to walk on a leash. Please don't let her go because she will run and hide, so if you put her on the ground, don't drop the leash." Gaby just nods. She is too excited to talk because ever since she first saw Peachy and all she represents, she has felt a knot in the middle of her throat.

The minute Gaby has Peachy in her arms; she knows this is the dog she is taking home. Angel and Ricardo try to persuade her to take a different dog, maybe one that is not so fearful, like Karina, since Karina has already bonded with Andrew and Fergie. But Gaby is determined to take Peachy. She puts Peachy on the ground and Peachy, of course, runs for cover. Gaby just goes after her and recovers her from underneath Angel's deck. Ricardo and Angel just look at the whole scene and shake their heads. After all, Gaby had been told not to put Peachy on the ground. But Gaby, through all the years she spent rescuing dogs on the streets of Mexico, have made her learn how to recover them from the strangest places. A deck is not going to stop her from getting Peachy back in her arms.

Peachy "The Warrior Princess"

The conversation about Peachy being fearful, not being housebroken, not being able to walk on a leash, not having many teeth, and all the other defects continued between Ricardo and Angel. They do their best to discourage Gaby from taking Peachy, but Gaby is not going to let Peachy stay at the rescue. She is determined to take her home. At the end of the interview Gaby and Ricardo leave the adoption ranch with two dogs, Peachy and Karina, for a sleepover and a day-trial. They will need to go back to the rescue ranch the next day to tell Angel if they will take both dogs or only one, and if only one, which one. They will need to get the adoption papers all finalized, too.

Ricardo and Gaby go straight from the rescue to the pet store to buy some dog supplies. They buy doggie diapers for Peachy, because the next day they will have to drive nine hours back home. Karina, Fergie and Andrew know how to let them know when they need to get out of the car, but little Peachy will mess up the car seat instead of asking to be let out to go to the bathroom. Ricardo and Gaby also buy some outfits for Peachy and toys for the other dogs.

They head back to the hotel and work on bonding with the dogs. Gaby also grooms Karina since Karina is in need of grooming. She promised Angel she would help with that. The night at the hotel is good; all the dogs sleep well in the bed with Ricardo and Gaby.

The next morning it's time for Ricardo to make a decision, because Gaby is determined to take Peachy and Ricardo likes Karina better. They realize they can't handle four dogs, so they will have to return one of the girls to the rescue group. Gaby says, "Ricardo, Peachy is the one that needs us the most, because she has been in the rescue organization for two years. Nobody wants her because she is too afraid. I can't let her live the rest of her life without knowing what a family is like. I also feel for Karina, but she has much better chances of finding a loving home." Ricardo agrees and off they go, back to the rescue to talk to Angel.

At the rescue, Angel is waiting for them and she is surprised to see Peachy walking on a leash. Because Gaby and Ricardo had managed to get Peachy to walk on a leash, that is the decision point for Angel. Angel thinks about Peachy leaving the ranch all curled up and fearful and how now, not even twenty-four hours later, she is walking on a leash and wagging her tail right along with a pack of three other poodles.

Gaby and Ricardo explain to Angel why they think four dogs will be too much for them and how sad they feel about leaving Karina with her, but Angel knows Karina is going to find a loving family more easily than Peachy. She decides it is time to sign Peachy's adoption papers so Gaby and Ricardo can drive back home with her.

It is bittersweet for Gaby and Ricardo, and definitely a hard decision, to leave Karina at the rescue, but Gaby knows Karina is going to be safe there and will have a loving home soon. Ricardo and Gaby start driving back home and Peachy sits in the back seat with Andrew and Fergie as if she has always travelled with them. Peachy has also started to follow Fergie everywhere and Fergie seems to have decided to take her under her wing and teach her all she knows about living life as a princess dog.

Peachy "The Warrior Princess"

On the way home, Gaby and Ricardo stop at a hotel about half way through the trip. This is to become the first of Peachy's many hotel experiences. Peachy decides she will sleep inside one of the night tables, because the night table has a hole with no door. So Gaby gives her one of the bed pillows and puts it in the hole so Peachy doesn't have to sleep all night on the hard wood surface of the night table. Peachy keeps from going potty all night and doesn't mess up the hotel room. She is being very good, but she is still not sure about Gaby and Ricardo. The only one she trusts is Fergie, so she decides to follow her around at every stop they make.

On the second day of the road trip they arrive home. Peachy gets to see for the first time the place where she will live. The house isn't big but it has lots of stairs since it was designed as a high-rise bungalow. Peachy's new challenge is to learn how to go up and down the stairs. She had a couple of accidents going down the stairs, and every time she does; she scares the soul out of Gaby's and Ricardo' bodies. They are so worried she will get injured. Peachy quickly learns how to go up the stairs, but she can't seem to learn how to go down the stairs. What she does learn is to wait to be picked up in loving arms and carried down the stairs.

With Peachy finally safe at home, Gaby realizes Peachy will breathe quickly and be kind of agitated while napping. Peachy dreams, and for sure those dreams are not good memories of her past life.

The time for Peachy's first vet appointment in her new home arrives. On her first veterinarian checkup, the vet tells Gaby that Peachy's five remaining teeth are not good, and that the two canine teeth on the bottom need to be pulled out since they are creating a problem. The teeth are so decayed and rotten that Peachy was getting an open sore on her chin. Gaby agrees they need to be pulled and the next day Peachy is put under for teeth removal and cleaning. When she wakes up, she starts looking for her canines with her tongue, running her tongue back and forth on her bottom gums. This impresses the nurses in the recovery room. They think it is very smart of Peachy to do that.

By now Peachy has spent a month in her new home. She has become quite an expert at riding in the car, although she is still very unsure of people, even of Ricardo and Gaby. She prefers to stay away from them and that makes Gaby's heart ache. Gaby starts looking for new ways to help Peachy recover from the entire puppy-mill trauma. Through Gaby's rescue friends she finds out about an animal communicator who has helped many rescue dogs settle in at their new homes. She decides to give it a try and books Peachy for and appointment with the animal communicator. Little does Gaby know that will be the beginning of a healing journey for her, too?

Peachy shows some improvements after her consultation with the animal communicator and Gaby is so surprised that she decides to explore more about energy healing and animal communication. Peachy has a couple more session with the animal communicator and every time she improves more and more. She starts barking, and she is feeling and being more confident every day. By November 2008, Peachy decides she would like to join Fergie and be a therapy dog. For that she needs to be certified so she can visit the elderly people at the retirement home. Peachy tells her animal communicator that Fergie has told her all about the visits and Peachy thinks it is a cool job to visit the elderly people and help them feel happier.

The day of the Therapy dog testing arrives and Peachy passes the test. She excelled, even though she was still a little bit shy. Before long, Peachy starts visiting seniors and she does that job for about two years. She really enjoys visiting, because she knows she will get pet and she'll get treats from the seniors. Since she is so small, she knows they will all want to have her on their lap.

Peachy also starts traveling once a year with her family to the veterinary specialist clinic in Michigan to take Andrew, her brother, to see the eye doctor. Andrew has glaucoma and cataracts, so his eyes need to be checked every year to ensure the medication is working.

Peachy has become an expert traveler. She sleeps on the back seat of her family's SUV with Fergie and Andrew. Peachy barks to let her parents know she needs to do a bathroom stop. She learned all this from imitating and watching Andrew and Fergie.

Peachy is also being seen at the specialist clinic. Since she spent so long in a puppy-mill, Gaby wants to make sure her eyes are doing okay. Once, she was seen by a liver doctor since her regular doctor thought her liver was getting enlarged.

When Peachy had the liver issue in 2009, Gaby decided Peachy was not going to be put on conventional medication, because the conventional medication on the market would kill her in the long run. Instead, Gaby contacted a Natural Veterinarian so Peachy got her liver problem treated with natural medication. As a result, Peachy is a healthy happy little girl.

Peachy has improved a lot and she is food-driven for sure, but her confidence has improved immensely. Now she is close to her family and she gets close to human visitors as well as dog visitors. She is called The Guardian because every time she hears the door, she will get up from her bed and run to the stairs that lead to the main entrance to bark at whoever is on the other side of the door. We believe Peachy is a happy girl now.

Conclusion

Peachy was only five pounds but she was five pounds of love and happiness. She has moved out of the fear and shattered world of puppy-mills and out of her puppy-mill traumas and memories to become a little funny dog. She had physical limitations but that did not stop her from trying every single thing the world threw at her. She learned how to go upstairs despite her leg issues; she would always ask you to try whatever you were eating despite having only one canine and a molar on the left side of her mouth. She would do her happy dance at feeding time; and she ran as fast as she could to jump on her crate to be fed, despite knowing her legs sometimes failed and she would slip and fall; she learned how to use her nose despite not being unable to use her nose for nearly eight years. She had learned to bark to let her people, Gaby and Ricardo, know what she needed, despite having lived in silence for many, many years at the puppy mill and having to relearn how to bark. She also will happily go for walks, even though her front legs will quit on her several times during the walk and she would go face down on the grass. As soon as that happened she got up as fast as she could and kept on walking.

The past six years of Peachy's life had been a learning curve, and she showed courage and determination. She learned a lot through imitating the other dogs and she was determined to live the rest of her life to the fullest. Regardless of her early trauma and all the physical limitations she carried because of those dark years at the puppy mill. Peachy was a warrior and today I can say she is probably the one that rescued me. We always get what we need, and I got an abused, shattered little dog that taught me to get up, no matter what the situation may be. To get up and live life to the fullest that is Peachy's lesson for us.

Peachy's story is a story with many lessons. I have rescued many dogs in my life and have never rescued a dog that would take years to recover and one who would recover so slowly; one that at the beginning did not want to be touched at all. Ricardo, who was originally against getting Peachy, is now madly in love with her and surprised at how much she has changed. Peachy made a 180-degree change for the better and was the happiest of all girls. She was truly a warrior.

Because everything was so new for her, Peachy had a couple close calls. She had to go to emergency care twice, but both times she fought back because she knew she had many years to still enjoy the sweetness of life. She has also been treated energetically for her seizures and as I suspected, her seizures were related to emotions stuck on her energetic body. When she got overloaded she would have seizures. Conventional medicine was not able to help her with this, since all the seizure medicines on the market are just like anesthetics. In the long run they affect other organs and end up killing the seizure patient.

The most recent trip Peachy made was December 2012, when she went with her family to Mexico to spend the holidays with Gaby's parents. Of course Gaby and Ricardo knew Peachy was a pro traveling on land, but they never realized she would do so well going in a little carrier under the seat in the airplane. Peachy was not alone, she was with her teacher Fergie who also made the trip, but still Peachy excelled, traveling from northern Ontario to Mexico is not an easy trip it usually takes 3 airplanes. We decided to drive to Detroit in order to reduce the stress to only two airplanes but still it was a 10 hour day thru airports and airplanes and our little Peachy did not even care, she slept the whole time. We got down to Veracruz; spent three 3 weeks there and came back to Canada. Peachy behaved like a professional frequent flyer. That also made our move to Alberta easier.

In February 2013, Fergie, Andrew and Peachy moved to Calgary Alberta with their family and now they have a new group of veterinarians that care for them. Peachy had a rough start this year since she had a little nasal discharge and she was not doing well for a while.

I honestly thought we were going to lose her. The doctors did not know what exactly was causing it, and Peachy was having seizures, did not want to eat, she slept all the time, etc. Well, again we had to contact her animal communicator to make sure if this was the end. We thought we were going to make the decision of helping her go, something I'm not comfortable doing but after the session with the animal communicator we learned it was not her time and Peachy regained strength. She started eating again and being in a better place. So we decided to wait for her to recover and later in May she ended up having her last two teeth pulled. It turned out she had some roots in her gums causing an infection that gave her a nasal discharge. She survived surgery and she did great.

Peachy was definitely a warrior and at 13 years old was an example for us to never give up, I truly believe she loved life, and enjoyed being alive, that's why she kept defeating illnesses and challenges.

I believe she would wake up giving thanks for being alive, and safe in a loving family and ready for whatever curve ball life would decide to throw at her every day, her attitude towards life was to live it to the fullest as long as she could, and she let us know, every morning at 6a.m., when she entered, the bedroom and started going around our bed looking for any sign of us been awake so we would serve her breakfast, LOL.

Her happiest times of the day were breakfast and dinner when she ran towards us, and circle around our legs while we were preparing her dish. After, she ran frantically to her crate where we would hang her dish. She knew the routine and she hardly ever went in her crate. Her crate was only used to hang her dish so she could eat sitting. This made it easier for her legs since her legs were a little wobbly at times.

The intention of sharing Peachy's life story is to touch at least a million kids and their families and in doing so, being able to raise awareness about the importance of adopting a dog and why we should never buy dogs from pet stores or backyard breeders.

There are millions of dogs that are put down every year at shelters. They wait in rescue organizations around the world for a forever home, sometimes never making it out. That would have been Peachy's case. When we met her, she had been abused so badly that despite been a little dog with an unusual color that anybody would want, she was too afraid to go home with anyone. She had decided that the rescue organization was better than going home with a family. She had learned that she could only trust one person and that was the rescue. Sometimes, when adopting a pet we need to look above and beyond their outer shell. What Peachy was telling me the day we met her was, "I'm too afraid to go to a home; I've been sabotaging my adoption to a family for the past two years. Please leave me alone. I want to die in this safe place."

But I knew I needed to get her out of there and show her what love and a loving family is like. It sure was a challenging ride, but I'm glad we adopted Peachy and I'm happy to share her story with you. In doing so, I hope to open your hearts to adopting a dog and open your eyes to the hidden and dark world of puppy-mills

When adopting, please see beyond the fear in the dog's eyes. It's rewarding to work with an abused dog and change a life. After all, that's what we come to the world for—to make a better world for all living beings including ourselves and our beloved families.

Some resources on finding a pet are

Visit your local shelter. There are many purebred, as well as many small or large mixed breeds that are waiting for homes. When adopting, take some time to know the dog. Bring all your family members, including your pets, to meet the new dog you are thinking about adopting. This will ensure a successful adoption. If the shelter doesn't have the dog you are looking for, ask if they have a waiting list and put your name down for a dog. Many shelters keep waiting lists and will notify you if the breed you want comes in to the shelter.

Look online at **petfinder.com, adopt a pet.com** and **1800saveapet.** These are three of the many wonderful databases you can find, and all you have to do is go online and fill in six boxes. The website will search for the dog you want and throw back at you pages and pages with dogs that match your search in the area where you live or nearby. If nothing that comes back interests you, you can sign up for reports so the database will keep looking for the dog you want. Twice a week they will email you with matches for your search.

Check for local nonprofit rescue organization, shelters, humane societies and reputable breeders in your area. Many times the breeders will have dogs that have been returned to them because their families can't have them anymore. A responsible breeder will take the dog back no matter how long ago they sold the dog and they will find this dog a forever home with a loving family.

Last but not least, if you want a purebred dog with papers, you can always go to the specific breed club and look there for rescues or reputable breeders. Breeders often have retired show dogs that they would love to send to a forever home, often at no cost or just for the cost of neutering or spaying. One example is www.poodleclubofamerica.com. Once there, go in to the rescue section. I really believe that if you want a pet, any dog will do, the only reason to get a pedigree puppy is if you are involved or want to explore the world of dog shows and dog competitions.

Gabriela Duran

And most recently I bumped in to a wonderful website where you can adopt a puppy mill survivor, <u>www.milldogrescue.org</u>. I just thought to throw this at you, in case you want to share your life with one of these wonderful dogs.

I hope this all will help you and we can start making a difference, reducing the amount of unwanted pets in the world. I'm forever thankful that you took the time to pick up this book and read it.

Many blessings,
Gaby and Peachy

Part II

For teens, young adults and adults. With my entire heart, I hope this inspires you.

When I started writing this book my intention was and still is to touch kid's hearts and start opening their eyes to the hidden world of puppy mills. I believe knowledge is power and believe that kids have the power to turn around the messed up world that we live in. I also believe younger generations are coming into this world with a higher consciousness and a deeper awareness of what we came to this world with, only because the times we are living in now requires it.

In this second part of the book I want to touch older kids and adults because I believe Peachy's story can touch the hearts of all of us not only kids and I also believe that Peachy has survived many things in life for a reason. She came into this world with a mission. Peachy has been our greatest teacher. She has changed our lives so much. Ricardo and I often marvel at her, at how much she has endured and changed, and still how much she keeps surprising us every day, she is truly a warrior with a message in her story and that's why we decided to help her spread her word. As stated before I'm only the helper, she is the Teacher.

Despite all her physical challenges, she is full of light. She does get herself into the silliest predicaments that any "well raised" dog would easily resolve. I'm not saying she is not smart, because I do believe dogs are very smart and in all my years as a proud poodle Mom, crazy dog lover and rescuer I can say that poodles are one of the smartest dogs I have ever seen, but I have also learned how early exposure and being raised in a loving home helps dogs get smarter. Peachy some days will get herself in a two wall corner and will not know how to get out of there. Something any of my other dogs would easily resolve. Peachy starts backing up, and tries to turn around sometimes hitting herself with the walls; we of course help her by picking her up and getting her out of her predicament. But like this, she will turn into a wall or fall off couches and steps, (she has no sense of depthness, since it's said that dogs develop their sense of depthness by experimenting around the house as puppies and falling off steps in their early months of existence, opportunity she never had, living in a cage at the mill all her puppy life).

Before adopting Peachy I was probably a dog snob. Even though I have always rescued and rehomed dogs, the dogs in my possession where pedigree, show champion dogs, I was a hard core believer on the American Kennel Club, and trained at my local Kennel club. So I raised my dogs to be the perfect companions and champions. My dogs where never to mess up in the house or their crate, yes their crate, because even though my dogs where not the typical show dog who spends his/her entire life in the crate or kennel run, my dogs had crate time during the day. Feeding time will be done in a crate, and if they were getting a little unease they would get timed out in their crate. I'm not saying this is wrong. In fact, I'm still a believer of crate training my dogs. Having my dogs crate trained made my life so much easier when I moved from Mexico to Canada. But maybe the next time I get to raise a puppy, if I ever get a puppy again (my heart is truly set on older dogs that no one wants), I will be wiser and I will raise the perfect companion instead of the perfect show dog/companion.

Peachy has also taught me to slow down. You see in my life as a dog rescuer/ dog re-homer/ dog trainer I was not exactly very patient, and I never needed to be patient because dogs will just follow me, until I got Peachy, who as I explained, wanted nothing to do with me or my husband. Peachy was truly terrified of us or any human. She had warmed up to the rescue lady who I called Angel in the story, but they really did not have a bond. Peachy truly did not know how to bond with a human nor was interested on learning. Humans were not to be trusted.

At this point all my rescuer experience was worth nothing. Peachy did not care if I had years of experience rescuing dogs from the streets in Mexico, working with "aggressive" dogs at the shelter in Canada, training dogs for obedience and agility trials with my kennel club friends, evaluating dogs to be therapy dogs, having dogs since I can recalled, or had a master's degree and loved dogs all my life. She just did not care. For her I was another human not to be trusted. I had to learn to breath and be patient. I had to slow down because with any sudden movement Peachy would run for cover. Sometimes risking her own life.

For her a crate was a safe place, we did provide her with a wire crate (I like wire crates because dogs can see around them when they are crated, they also get more light and air in a wire crate), and even though we never crated her, the crate was there for her to go in and feel safe if she wanted to, after all, she had spent five years in a puppy mill crate and two years in a rescue crate, so all she knew was crates.

We also provided her with a collar and a tag that I ended up removing the first week after she had her ID tag caught in the crate (super scary moment), and of course she did not know what to do so she just kept pulling until I was able to get her collar off. What exactly happened was, I walked to close to her and she panic, rushing into her crate for cover, jumping inside and getting her ID tag caught on it. Thankfully I was there to help her but the incident scared the soul out of me and I decided she was not going to wear a collar and tag because she could get caught on something else and eventually die trapped or asphyxiated.

I really had to re-learn all my rehabilitation dog methods that I had used in the past. She was different to an abandoned, stray or a feral dog, and I had to start looking into her eyes more and try to read her. This was not easy, If you look at dogs eyes, you can almost see their souls and with this you can determine if the dog is going to let you help it or not. The eyes of my other dogs read different. With Andrew you can tell by looking at his eyes he is a spicy dog. He likes to have fun and do his own thing. He likes to get in trouble. Fergie, you can see the wisdom in her eyes. She is an old soul. You can't really punish her. If she gets in trouble. She looks at you like saying "you are wrong, it's part of life and who I am, I'm ok" she is super friendly and full of kindness. Our little Peachy all you could get from reading her eyes was "stay away from me, I'm so shattered and fearful, humans are not to be trust". This of course crushed my heart. Almost for a year that was all you could get from her eyes.

And every time I picked her up, her heart was pumping so hard that it felt like she would almost have a heart attack.

The first time I got her to lay down on the couch was the summer of 2007 a couple weeks after we got her, and she only stayed on the couch because Andrew and Fergie where there with me, but she was breathing so fast her little chest was rising up and her eyes were moving, she was sleeping and I do believe she was having nightmares, for the longest time every time she fell asleep she would breath rapidly, it was almost like she was not resting at all.

In the summer of 2008 we got her to sleep in bed with us, since Fergie my other poodle has always slept in bed with me and later when I married she taught my husband he was the intruder in bed and despite all his efforts to keep her out of bed, it only took one night of Fergie jumping to be put on the bed for him to understand he needed to get used to having her in bed with us. Ricardo is a dog lover too (otherwise I would have never marry him), but for some reason he did not want her in bed with us. Anyhow, when we got Peachy; well Peachy was so attached to Fergie that the first night at home she could not sleep because she was looking for Fergie. Fergie was in bed with us and Peachy ended up in bed with us within a couple of weeks. Getting Peachy in bed was not an easy task, after all this dog had not sense of depthness, did not trust us and had never slept in a bed in her life.

We took some precautions after she almost fell of the bed, we bought some cheap foam mattress covers that we used to roll every night on each side of the bed to cushion her fall in the event of her falling. She did fall off a couple times; our bedroom was carpeted as well as the rest of the house but that also changed in time, carpet and dogs don't mix well specially if one of your dogs is a puppy mill rescue who has zero house training and who of course is going to release herself in the carpet if she gets nervous, so carpet had to go, Peachy was only the confirmation for us that carpet needed to go. My other two dogs even though they were house trained and clean every time they got nauseous they would puke on the carpet, so since we got the house we knew carpet needed to go sooner or later, plus I'm sort of allergic to carpets too, but that is not really as important, LOL.

Because we had Peachy in bed with us we were able to notice in that summer that during thunderstorm season she would have seizures. Again another learning experience for me. I really considered myself a pretty tough lady who had seen enough horror during her years as a dog rescuer but having your own little five pound dog having a seizure in the middle of the night scared the soul out of me. The first time Peachy had a seizure I wanted to get her in my arms and drive to the veterinarian with her. It was horrible seeing this little five pound fur ball not being able to control her body and worse she did not understood what was going on. She was as scared as I was. In my life the only time I had seen someone having a seizure was when I was about nine years old and one of the house workers at my parents' house was epileptic and ended up having a seizure at work. I remember being impressed by the whole deal. Seeing my brothers picking him up from the floor, and getting him inside the house full of blood from hitting on asphalt. They also pulled his tongue with a spoon, like I said I was a little girl and I was scared so my mother pulled me away from the whole scene and the man was taken to the hospital. So, when Peachy started having a seizure I was beside myself but Ricardo had experience with this matter as his brother had epilepsy and he kept us both calm. He knew what was going on and said to me "there is nothing to do, but wait, just pet her, keep her calm and wait until it passes" (wait until it passes???, I was really thinking, you are crazy!!, this little girl is going to die on us, lets rush to the hospital), that summer we had a few thunderstorms and each time Peachy had a seizure during the storm in the middle of the night. I took her to the veterinarian, only to learn that there is nothing to do for animals with seizures and as long the seizures are no longer than a minute is better to avoid medications. The reason being that the current meds for seizures are sedatives. Sedatives like many other chemicals end up affecting other organs and in the long run killing the patient.

Learning about animal communicators and to open my mind

"You get in life what you need, I believe Peachy came to me because it was time to re-explore and learn more about natural healing, it was time to start my own healing journey".

Because of Peachy's new found seizures and her being still fearful of us after a year of living as a free dog and a beloved pet, I started exploring other methods to help her, without knowing I was also helping myself.

Well you see I was born in México and my family is not keen on surgery and medications. I had tons of troubles with my tonsils and I remember my father not letting any doctor remove them. Because he said and has been his experience "tonsils are there to protect the rest of the respiratory track and people that have no tonsils end up still getting sick but the infection goes into their tracchea and lungs creating other problems". So as sick as I was and as many times I had my tonsils infected I still have them, in fact the only surgery I have to overcome has been the wisdom teeth and only because it was absolutely necessary. I had such horrible after surgery experiences that I got the wisdom teeth pulled six months and a year apart from each other, and to this day I hope to never ever have any surgery again. So I should thank my parents for not letting the doctors remove my tonsils.

My parents, especially my mother, were always keen on looking for natural methods to heal illnesses and cleanse the body. I did see regular doctors but really some of my recurrent illnesses like tonsil infections and acne where not cured by these medical doctors. In fact they were cured by energy medicine and learning to take care of myself.

At the time Peachy was having all these issues in 2008, I did know that there was more than only regular medicine, but I was battling my own childhood issues, and looking for answers to my overwhelming feelings. Thankfully, I do have many good friends that are animal rescuers in México and in many other parts of the world and talking to one of them about Peachy and her seizures she said "why don't you try an animal communicator?" A what?

Even though I was raised by a mother that believes in spirits, natural healing, shamanism, and many other things; even though I was exposed to natural homemade remedies and saw one of my aunts heal from a varicose ulcer (that was so bad that you could see the bone on her ankle, and the chemicals and best specialist could not heal her) heal with pure and simple aloe Vera. And many other mysterious things that had happened in my parents' house that proof the spirit world exists. I had never heard about animal communication.

It's been said that in life you have many calls to awaken and one of my friends, a well know veterinarian, who I consider is very connected with her higher self also uses a lot of natural remedies, homeopathy and acupuncture to heal her patients especially because she helps many people that rescues dogs and have no money to pay for her services. So she has found natural medicine allows her to treat her patients at a lower cost and be gentler.

I was so blind because I was trained as a scientist, and I'm an Engineer with a Master in Sciences that was too scared to see more, so when my friend tried to introduce me to animal communication I was skeptic. But Peachy kept on having seizures, so I decided to give it a try.

As it turned out, this woman that was the first animal communicator in México was claiming to be able to communicate with your dog and heal your dog with energy. Well I decided to give it a try, after all Peachy was not going to be treated by chemicals, so I contacted the animal communicator in Mexico City and she treated Peachy long distance. Yes long distance. It's call distance healing but anyway, this lady gave me a report and said Peachy's seizures were purely emotional and that the seizures where because somehow her system was getting overloaded and she would go into a seizure. Of course by now my husband believes I'm crazy, he is certain this woman is scamming people, and I don't blame him, I have taken my dog to "Doctor Doolittle". Inside me a voice said you are doing the right thing and another voice (probably my left brain) said "you are nuts, Gabriela, you are truly nuts, definitely you lost all your marbles, all this years of science to believe someone that claims can communicate and heal your animal without even seeing it, you are really losing it!".

To my surprise, Peachy started to improve after her session with this animal communicator. She not only stopped having seizures so frequently, she started to come around and started trusting us. So my curiosity and my scientific training pushed me into research. During research I learned this whole Dr. Doolittle thing of communicating with animals is possible, and that there is a lady in the USA that has been doing this for decades. She is also an author and a trainer and she trains people to communicate and heal animals. I also learned that the woman from Mexico was not just a "crazy" person that claimed to communicate with your dog. She had a University Degree and got interested in this world of natural healing after having worked with the native people in México and having spent time doing research with the native Mexicans, who still refuse to see doctors, and live way longer than any "civilized" Mexican. I also learned that she bumped into Penelope Smith books while living in Spain. After working with the natives in México, when she returned to the "civilized" world she felt overwhelmed and started looking for ways to heal. This took her to the world of animal communication and shamanism. Anyhow, still this sound crazy so talking to my rescuer friend I said "I still don't believe all this, I know my dog is doing way better but still this is too crazy to believe" so she invited me to an animal communication training session in México City by the same animal communicator that was treating my Peachy. Of course I'm living in Canada, but I never refuse an excuse to go to back home and visit family. Despite my husband disbelieve and his reluctance to it, I packed my bags and off I went to the seminar in México City (I also used the time to visit family).

I arrived in México City and was picked up by one of my cousin, who is 30 some years older than me and treats me like her daughter. In fact she has been in occasions more of a mother than my own mom. So we have a deep connection. She also believes in the spirit world, healers, shamans, mentalist, psiquics, etc., but when I told her about this course she said, "That's impossible, this woman has found a way to make money out of people ignorance". I said I was skeptic and as a scientist this was part of my research.

So the day of the training session, my friend who invited me picked me up, she knew I was skeptic, I rode with her to the seminar and sure enough this animal communicator lady look to me like a scam, I was very judgmental of looks and this woman had evolved enough to don't care about how she looked like. She dressed in earth friendly clothes and despite her Spanish inheritance; she dressed more like the native Mexicans. Long skirt and loose clothes. At that point in time I was thinking "here we go Gabriela, you travelled all this far just to verify this is a scam".

The group of people attending the seminar, to my surprise, where all professionals. Many of them where veterinarians, other were lawyers, marketing specialist, engineers, scientist, but they all had one thing in common. The love for the animals. They also were looking for methods to heal themselves so we had a lot in common. I could totally relate to this group of people.

The seminar was a two day long seminar, the first day was mainly so you can practice the ability to communicate telepathically with each other, human to human and open your mind to the possibility of communicating without using your words. Then on the second day we brought in animals. By the time I took the seminar I had read both Penelope Smith books and it stuck to me that we have the ability to communicate with all the living things in the world. We are born with that ability but because the world sees people that claim to communicate with animals and telepathically as freaks, our parents raise us to be "normal". Shut down this ability and be disconnected. Penelope Smith also explains in her book Animal Talk, all the troubles she had to overcome, to accept the communication with animals is possible, exist and thanks to her today there are many animal communicators/ healers working to help our beloved fur babies.

I now believe the seminar facilitator was so connected that she knew I was a total skeptic and not only that, I was also cynical, so she kept on asking me questions throughout the whole seminar. I almost felt she was focused on me. To make me believe, at the time I was so disconnected and so hurt, I mean I had many emotions stuck from childhood, and living in Canada had only made that worse because for the first time in many years I had nothing to do, I was mainly volunteering and all my schooling was useless where I lived, because I was not certified by a Canadian Institution. So I spent a lot of my time at home, volunteering for the humane society and trying to start a business, and all the repressed feelings I had from childhood took the opportunity to surface and overwhelmed me. The animal communicator lady let's give her a name Maria, knew there was a lot going on in my life, but she also knew I needed to experience animal communication to be able to believe in it.

The first day was not special at all for me, we did some telepathy exercises with humans and I was not thrilled, a lot of the people there where beyond themselves and had to take brakes to process it, but on day two, when the people attending the seminar brought their pets, that was a whole different day. I was still skeptic and cynical but animals where there and to me animals are very important. I don't know if it's because I was raised with dogs, and I was fortunate to have many other pets, parrots, turtles, birds, bunnies, a cat, turkey, chickens; or because every single time I felt lonely as a child my dog was there with me to make it all better.

So day two here we go!, we started by going deep within through breathing exercises and then the real deal start trying to connect with the animals, (by then we were sitting in a circle surrounded

Peachy "The Warrior Princess"

by pet carriers or kennels) and each of us had our turn to bring an animal out. The ones, like me, who could not bring a pet, where asked to bring a picture of it, I of course had a picture of Peachy handy.

The thing that struck me the most was many Veterinarians who were taking the seminar, had stories about hearing their patients talking to them. These Veterinarians mainly worked with horses in not so busy city environments. That day, I was still cynical so Maria the teacher would ask us to communicate with the animal and then she would ask us "who wants to share!" everyone was excited and raising their hands but not me. I was in my scientific, cynical, skeptic, etc., self so, she would ask me directly. I kept answering what I got as a message. The one animal that impressed me the most was this little schnauzer mix that belonged to a lawyer friend of mine and had been rescued from the streets of Mexico City. She was very alert and happy to be in class, so it got to the point that even though it was not her turn yet to participate, we were asked to communicate with her. She showed us about her rescue and how thankful she was of having been rescued. But I saw something else.

Of course Maria knew I had seen something else, or should I say I had received more information from this dog, so she pushed me to tell her what I saw. I said "I saw the same thing everyone else" of course I was lying and Maria knew it, she said "you saw something else, please share with us", I reluctantly started saying that this dog showed me a garage with a big rod iron door and the car parking outfront. She getting off the door and running down the street and then she showed me asphalt like a brand new asphalted street with lots of traffic. Many cars going up and down the street, the dog stopped near traffic sign and decided to cross the street, finding herself sitting in the middle of traffic not knowing what to do. Maria said what else, I said that's it because my dog keeps popping in, Maria replied is it a white poodle looking dog? With a red toy? I said yes, Maria replied I was going to ask who the owner of this dog is because since yesterday he keeps coming to me. He has a message. I was beyond myself, how does this woman know I had another dog. I mean she knew I had Peachy and had treated her but I never mentioned Andrew. She also knew about Fergie because Peachy had told her about but not Andrew and how was it possible that Andrew, in Canada, was trying to get into this animal communication course. How did he know what his mom was up to? In the meantime, of course the owner of the schnauzer was beyond herself wrapped in guilt and crying, she said to us that the image her dog showed me was the time she had been a neglectful owner and being so wrapped in life that when coming back from the supermarket, she opened the door and did not realize the dog had ran away. She felt mega guilty because she felt she had rescued the dog only to get it killed hit by a car. While she was telling us the story wrapped in guilt and crying her dog was very impatient, acting up and looked uncomfortable, so Maria said that the dog had brought it up because she knew her human hated herself because of this issue and she wanted her human to forget about it. It was only an accident and she was fine after all.

Anyway, believe it or not, after I acknowledged that my dog kept popping in every time we were communicating with an animal, he just did it more and not only that, because we were not communicating with him, he brought his sisters in to the picture, I know it sounds crazy, but It did happen and you will only understand it by having this experience. Andrew is much attached to me and very possessive so it was only OK for him to intrude on the animal communication exercise. Maria also said he's almost selfish and that's why Peachy is not interested on him. Peachy describes Andrew as a spoiled rotten dog that wants everything for himself. Peachy once said on a follow up communication/healing session in 2009, "I don't like that Andrew dog, I don't like his energy".

Well after all Andrew came to my life after I had tragically lost my three previous dogs. He is also the first dog with papers (pedigree) I ever got. The first dog I did obedience, agility and conformation with and he was also the only dog in my life for about a year so all the attention was for him. He received lots of praise and encouragement for all the things he did in the show rings and at home. He's a proud boy and he also has exhibit signs of being protective of me.

After the second day at the course, the communications with the animals and all the testimonials from the Veterinarians in class I had to do more research and started believing. This course was a life changing experience and the beginning for me, to explore the world of healing.

Meet the pack

Andrew

He was born as a strong free spirit and a leader, but I also recognize I did encourage him to be a strong minded dog. Andrew came to my life in a very critical moment. I was in University and my life, as I knew it, had changed. I was clearly suffering and in pain, feeling rejected by my family and not able to fit in with them. Also having a lot of school pressure, I had been a straight A student all my life and I was struggling to keep being that in University. To make matters worse I had been left without a dog for the first time in nineteen years. Since I can recall there had always been dogs in my life. I got my first own dog at age three, and before that there where at least two working dogs in the house at all times due to my father's passion for hunting.

But six months before Andrew arrived my dog had been stolen and because he was the third dog that had either gotten lost, tragically died or taken in the past couple years, my father decided I was not allowed to have another dog.

I was under tons of stress due to family issues and school and now I was also dog less, life was truly over for me, remember, I was only nineteen. I knew I had to get myself another dog, but the question was how? I did not have a job or money to buy myself a dog and adoption where I lived was not an option. There weren't any rescue groups in my city, and at the animal control facility all dogs that came in there were killed so I decided to enroll my aunt. She gave me the money for the dog. Technically my dad gave me the money because my aunt was dad's sister who lived with us and sort of controlled the books for my dad's business. She was reluctant at first, but I convinced her to go see the puppies that I had found in the newspaper add with me. That was it, who says no to puppies?

Peachy "The Warrior Princess"

We went to visit the breeder in a house with lots of poodles; this woman was a lawyer who was deep into poodles. She had all colors and sizes, and she had been into dog shows for a while. All of this was new to me. Anyway we went inside the house, saw the dogs, they were all running around free, healthy and looked happy. This woman also took the time to talk to us, researched us, asked me why I wanted a dog, where I was planning to keep the dog?, What I was planning to do with the dog?, Why I wanted a poodle?, Why was I interested on a pure breed dog?, etc. She showed us all the dogs she had as breeding stock, the dogs were running around the house so she had to call them to be able to show them to us, showed us the dogs papers, where they came from, how they were kept and on and on. I do remember that we visited this woman about three times before I got to pick up Andrew. She seemed to be very concern about who she sold her dogs to. I also learnt that pure breed dogs come with a guarantee, meaning the breeder will take the dog back if it is ill at any stage of the dog's life and replace it for you if the dog is sick or dies.

In one of the visits she showed us a little poodle a "tea cup poodle", because at that point, even though I had always had poodles, I heard a lot about tea cup poodles and I wanted a small tiny little poodle and this breeder educated me. She told me that tea cup poodles are "poodles with dwarfism" that they can be born in a litter of normal miniature or toy poodles and more than been sold more expensive because of their little size, they should be placed in good homes and whoever the parents (meaning the sire and dam) of this little "tea cup" dog are should be fixed and never be bred again. But because a lot of people wanted smaller and smaller dogs many breeders were and still are breeding to obtain smaller dogs (not necessarily healthy dogs), which is the whole propose of getting a pure breed dog from a breeder, to ensure you are getting not only the dog according to the AKC breed standard, but a healthy dog, bred in a cruelty free environment, also in the case of poodles a dog that has a good temperament not a crazy, barky one.

Gabriela Duran

She said to me that the little "tea cup" poodle, well she called it by its name the little dwarf poodle, that had been born from one of her litters of puppies was not going to be sold. She was looking for the perfect family for her and I was clearly not a match. She wanted someone that would take this dog with her/him everywhere and pay total and complete attention to this dog. The dog was a red "tea cup" female but as many of these "tea cups" she was missing teeth. The breeder also explained to me these dogs often are born missing reproductive organs and that she did not understand why people where so into getting an unhealthy dog creating the demand for breeders to start breeding "tea cups". Anyhow she was very honest and at the time her dogs where a little more of want my aunt and myself wanted to pay for a dog, after all, all my dogs in the past have come to me as a gift and the only one that had been bought at a veterinary clinic not even a pet store, had died tragically as a puppy, after much suffering due to a heart defect. Having been taken from his mom way too early and a tail crop badly done, leaving me and my family broken hearted. I vowed then that I was never going to buy another dog, unless I did my homework.

So when time came to get Andrew I felt I had done my homework. I made sure the breeder was good, that there was no cruelty involved with the breeding dogs, that the breeding dogs where living as pets, and so on, but that came at a price I could not pay. It was only 300 dollars for a full pedigree, full guarantee dog but to my aunt that was way too much money and to me well I did not have any money so I was not in a position to discuss. Because we kept going back to the breeder and asking her questions she ended up telling me, she was going to have a litter of pups that where cheaper, because they had half pedigree's. To me really a pedigree meant nothing, I just wanted a healthy dog and if possible a dog that was accepted at the local kennel club so I could start learning obedience and agility training. The breeder explained that this litter had the complete four generations on the father side but only a couple generations of information on the mother side so that made them a pure breed with half pedigrees. Therefore cheaper dogs and she could not guarantee them because she did not know if there were any genetic diseases in these dogs' lines.

She could sell us one of these pups for half the price. Still too much money to pay for a dog but my aunty agreed to give me the money so I could have a dog. We paid half that day and the other half was to be paid on pick up day. The pups will be ready to leave their mom three months after been born, so we agreed and that worked for me since that was Christmas vacations and I could pick the dog on the last day of school.

The last day of school, I went after classes to pay and pick Andrew up from the breeder, I have to admit, she had gotten him all cleaned up in a poodle puppy cut, she did care about her dogs and that was the way she showed it. She also said if I had any questions I could call her anytime. She told me what kind of brush to get and where to get it and asked me if I had a doggie bed. I had come with a doggie hoodie since it was winter time and this pup was leaving his birth place forever. So I covered him up and took him home.

Andrew was the tiniest dog, the runt of the litter and many of my family members thought I had been scammed again. That the dog was too young and was going to die, totally not true, Andrew had full dentures, was eating kibble by himself, trained to pee on pee pads, and true he was tiny but he was not lame, he was very alert, he came home and started playing with the toys I had for him. Despite my half siblings coming asking if he had passed every time they came home, Andrew was growing strong, he was alert and happy, something my late puppy did not have, my aunt and I had done our research this time. Yeah us!

Andrew is now a mature wise man, he's fifteen years old and still going strong, he takes his heart meds every day, eats well, and takes care of his body by resting enough, he also still plays a lot, loves toys and even though he's blind he has learned to listen so If you ever see him out with the girls (Fergie and Peachy), you will never guess he's blind until you get a chance to look at his eyes. He has learned to use his other senses, to keep going and live with his disability. He has learned to listen to my voice when he is out for a walk or needs to do stairs. We don't baby him or duel on his blindness, we or should I say, I have taught him he can still get around, and he has learned to yelp for help if he finds himself in a situation where he needs a guiding voice. This mainly happens when he is upstairs and needs to go down, he will yelp so you know he needs help and wait for you to come and guide him down with your voice, How?, I stand at the end of the stair case and tell him "step, step, step, another one, other one, last one, good boy", so he knows when there is no more steps, he surprisingly does not take the next step until he hears my voice and once he is on solid floor you can see him wag his tail is almost like he thanks you and at the same time he's proud that he made it. He also responds to words like "careful" because sometimes when going on a walk he is on full speed, walking on a leash and we are aware we are his eyes, so, when we say careful he knows there is something ahead of him, like a wall or a sidewalk, or a step so he stops and waits to be guided.

I guess my whole point on bringing up Andrew's blindness and heart issues is, when adopting a pet don't let the "disability" on a pet fool you. Dogs pretty much guide themselves with their noses so being blind means nothing to them. Andrew still plays ball and Kong's, he has a huge wooden box full of toys and he knows where his favorite toy is by getting into the box and smelling them. He will always get out the box his favorite toy, a yellow bone like rubber toy, he has had since he was a puppy. Andrew's blindness and heart condition is congenital, is the (as I called it) "half pedigree" factor. He has a genetic disease called progressive thinning of the retina which is common in pure breed poodles and causes blindness, that's why AKC dogs are require to be eye certified, something I learned after by studying more about dog breeds. He also was born with a heart murmur for what he takes meds, now a days he's on what the vets like to call "Heart failure", and I know many people would had put him down long time ago, but that's just not us. He still wants to live and as long as he wants to stay with us, he's welcome.

Some days I believe there is no coincidence in him being blind, I do have myopia that I developed when I was eight years old and thru my energy medicine studies and reading of Louis Hay books, I learned that people with bad eyes is because we don't want to see. I probably did not want to see many things happening around me during my childhood, but I have always believed that animals take illnesses that come our way because their love for us is so unconditional that they rather be sick themselves.

And just recently I learned east Indian traditions believe that too, that's why some east Indians will keep fish tanks in their homes, because they believe that if there is any bad energy or disease coming their way the fish will intercept it and die first before this affects the family. Interesting eh!; so perhaps Andrew took the blindness that was coming my way and the heart murmur is maybe caused by him protecting me from being broken hearted, or maybe is just a congenital defect as western medicine has diagnosed it.

Fergie

Miss Fergie is a full pedigree girl who comes from show champions and her real name is D'Croda (breeder's name) Il Amore Di Fergie. She was born in a different breeding house and that was because I wanted a red poodle. Red poodles are not easy to find, especially in México, because in the dog show world black poodles and white poodles are more appreciated than any other color. That's why you will mainly find white poodles everywhere, a few blacks but almost none of the other six solid colors poodles come in, not counting the many party colors they also come in, yes I know they are dogs not cars or nail polish, but it's important to let the world know poodles come in many more colors than only black and white. As well as it was important to let the world know the origin of "tea cup poodles". Poodles also come in three different sizes, the original one the standard poodle and from those wonderful standards the smaller ones where bred to create the miniatures and the toys.

This shrinking of the breed happened many years ago in Europe and is been said that the French where the ones that decided to shrink the breed to make it more suitable for apartment living, due to the greatness of the breed, poodles are brilliant minds in dog disguises. The breed is originally from Germany and was a working breed. The standard poodles where hunting/retrieving dogs, that's why they have the coat trim with the pom poms. They used the poodles to retrieve in water. The show cut was created in the early days to protect mayor organs and joints on the dogs while they were doing their job, but enough history on the great poodles that I love so much!

Fergie is a beautiful old soul, in a beautiful red miniature poodle disguise. She is all kindness, friendliness and happiness. She is also in the AKC/FCI eyes a perfect specimen of the breed, and a multi show champion. You see when I got Fergie I was very into conformation and obedience competitions, Andrew was my only show dog at the time and he just did not enjoy it. He hated been brushed and being in a show cut, he was truly miserable. I have pictures of him in his show cut and just by looking on his eyes you can tell he hated me for having him in a show cut and made him go to dog shows with a handler (my biggest mistake ever). But I did enjoy doing things with my dogs and brushing them out. One day at a dog show I was introduced to Fergie's breeder.

My first poodle ever, the kindest dog I have had was a red toy poodle by the name of Charlie who was given to me as a gift and who made me fall in love with the breed. I have only good memories about him. I was five years old when I got him. Charlie and I went everywhere together. He ate anything I was eating and he was fed chicken wings and soup made fresh every day. He also was an older boy when he came to me. He was given to my half-brother who did not want him and gave him to me, but Charlie came knowing many tricks. He was never trained or anything, he was not even fixed but he knew not the get off the sidewalks, he knew that if he got out of the house and no one noticed, he would go to the front door and scratched it so someone would open the door for him. Charlie was smart beyond believe and he was the first dog my mother allowed me to keep as a pet. He lived inside the house, went with us everywhere, slept in bed with me, hated the veterinarian and knew the sound of the vet's car. So when he heard the vet car approach he ran for cover, the vet used to come to see Charlie at home, and the groomer also came home to see him. Charlie was spoiled but I was only a kid so I did my best to keep him happy and healthy, most of his care was my mother's responsibility, and Charlie lived a long life until sadly he could no longer walk and mother put him down. To me it was terrible and I fought and delayed the euthanasia as long as I could but I was helpless, loosing Charlie was to me like losing a brother, and my best friend.

So going back to Fergie, due to all the good memories about male red poodles I wanted another one. I did not have good memories about female poodles, because as a child and because Charlie was not fix my parents bred him, (you know to fulfill the "dog's needs"), whatever dogs don't really need to reproduce to be happy. We got a female by the name of Daisy and she was evil. She was white and evil. She hated me from day one. She would bite me. She was the classic neurotic poodle. She even fought the neighbor's dog, that was a Dalmatian mix, and Daisy won the fight, the poor Dalmatian was left unable to use her right front paw ever again because Daisy ripped off one of her pads. Of course the Dalmatian defended herself and grabbed Daisy by the neck. Daisy screamed hard enough that my mother came to rescue her and she only had a little scratch on the neck that healed in matter of days. Daisy was also put down due to old age. She went blind and mother who is not a dog lover decided to euthanize her. Mother still believes that was the kindest thing to do but I differ, you see Daisy was euthanized at home and she was clearly not ready to go. She was old and probably a month before being put down she had pups, which all died because she was an old dog, blind, unable to take care of them and the pups where premature. I did try to hand feed them and saving them, but one by one all died. We did not even know how she got pregnant, neither had we known she was pregnant, and after all her pups died well mother decided it was time to put her down. That dog knew, and she fought the chemicals. I remember the vet saying he could not believe it, he had already overdose her and she was still alive, he ended up giving her a shoot in her heart to force her to go and he succeeded. I'm still traumatized and cannot believe mother was so cold blooded to do this, after all Daisy was very attached to my mother. Because of previous euthanasia experiences my old, blind guy is still alive, he eats well moves well, there is no point to sentence him to death, I'm not God and Andrew is clearly not ready to go yet, nor was Daisy.

Anyway going back to Fergie's breeder, he lived an hour and a half north of my hometown so after we talked at the dog show and I explained I wanted another red toy male poodle. He gave me his email and contact info so we could keep in touch and negotiate. He explained he had two litters of pups coming one in March and one in April. He said the ones in March where all sold but he could probably sell me one of the ones being born in April. He researched me and he decided to give me a female. I wanted a show dog and he said he was going to choose me one. Truly the way it works is, the owner of the sire has pick of the litter and they usually get the best dog, then the breeder gets the second best for themselves if they want to keep one dog from that litter and sell the left overs. So in a way Fergie was the left over. Her sister was kept by the breeder and the male went to the sire owners as a payment for the sires work impregnating the female (Fergie's mom) all three of them were destined to spend their lives as show dogs in the show rings. Then retire after becoming champion, get shaved down and start producing pups.

Yes I wanted Fergie to keep showing but she was not going to live in a crate as a show dog. How I ended up getting a female, as I explained I got the runt of the litter who turned out to be the best show dog of the three, she competed against her siblings and always won, Fergie is a beauty and she made it clear to me that she was born to be a star, the minute she put her little paws on the show ring at age three months old she won over all the puppies in her category at the dog show. Since then she loved it, won every single time, I also learned to keep a closer eye on the handler and trust him less, and later to find her a nicer handler.

If you happen to be in to dog shows, keep an eye on your handler. Often they mistreat the dogs. Andrew, for example, is not a fan of men and will not let a male handle him at a vet clinic or doggie daycare. I do believe is because of his show handler; I decided to retire Andrew, the summer I got Fergie, I took them to a dog show and at the same dog show we tested her, Andrew retired.

I have had her for a week and Fergie came into the ring with no previous experience taking first place in her class, it was clear to me she was born to show, she seemed to love the attention; Andrew on the other side was stressed out, had a nasty diarrhea, and was vomiting vile all this while he waited ready on the grooming table to get his turn on the show ring, that day I made the decision he needed to be retire, I was torturing my dog and if I would have known earlier how miserable he was I would have retired him earlier. I rather have a live dog, than a dead champion. Many show dogs don't get to enjoy retirement, they die of sudden unexpected illnesses due to stress.

The world of dog shows is very stressful for them and I have seen many champions collapse, get ill or die suddenly just when they are at the top of their game and about to retire. To many of this owner/breeder/ handlers this means nothing because for them is only another dog or worse is only another womb, but for the show dog owners/aficionados like me, this means everything, after all Fergie is my daughter (sorry my beloved Cesar Millan but that's how I feel about her, and yes she knows I'm the pack leader) LOL, and from the minute she got dropped off by the breeder in my house that July 19th 2000 she and I bonded. I vowed to protect her as I vowed to protect Andrew and Peachy and any of the dogs in my care, I know every single dog lover feels this way so do your homework, research your breeders, handlers and trainers, I would even go to the point of researching my groomer too. A lot of this "professionals" are mean to our beloved pooches.

I learned the hard way, after going to a dog show to see my dog Andrew and realize he was ill on the grooming table with his neck tied to the arm of the table so he could not sit and mess up his legs for the show and when he had that explosive diarrhea on the table the handler was prompt to moved Andrew's body so he did not get any of that diarrhea on his perfectly groomed show coat and yes Andrew was still tied by his neck high to the arm of the table while the handlers helper cleaned the table. I wonder how many more times I was not at the show and this happened or worse how many times Andrew was mistreated at the dog shows by the handler and helper or just not shown because they did not feel like grooming him and then Andrew made the trip and spent all the weekend stuck in a crate. I've been around dog show many years to know that not all is beauty so if you are showing your dog or training your dog keep a close eye on the people doing this for you.

Fergie being my second dog in the show circles suffered less, because I kept a closer eye on the handler. I asked him several questions, I only send her to one or two shows per semester and made sure the handler was transporting the dogs humanly. This handler had no vehicle and often car pooled with the kennel club people, but often for the handlers to be worth it to go to a dog show, they take way to many dogs six or seven sometimes ten and even though they bring a helper that amount of dogs is too many for them. Also they usually like to go out and get drunk after each day of showing so while your handler is having fun your dog is stuck in a kennel in a dirty motel with a bunch of dogs unsupervised. It has also happened that at big dog shows while the handler and the helper are at the show ring the dogs that are not showing are left at the grooming station unsupervised and often get stolen from their crates by people "watching" the show.

Fergie's first big dog show was Expocan in Mexico City in September 2001. Expocan is a show that used to run for three weeks, where only the best dogs competed. For Fergie's first dog show her handler had no transportation and too many dogs. He decided to ride the bus (by this I'm referring to a greyhound type of bus) from Veracruz to México city, well the dogs were shipped in cargo in the bus, of course because I was keeping an eye on him and by then I had just finished school, (I was waiting to graduate and go off to do my masters) I had all the spare time to keep an eye on him, well I did not give him Fergie, despite all the pressure he was putting on me because I knew he had no vehicle and had not yet defined his traveling arrangements. He liked to have the dogs with him at least two days before the shows so he could "prepare them", some dogs lived with him permanently, and this guy was the best handler in town and had been one of the best in México for a long time even recognized in the USA as a good Mexican handler. Anyway I kept telling him as long as I don't know how you are going to ride with the dogs you won't get my dog. Sure enough last minute the day before the show, I learned he was going on a bus and was taking the dogs in cargo. There was no way Fergie was going to travel with him, most dog owners to this day don't know their dogs were put in the cargo compartment of a bus for six hours Veracruz-México city trip in hot kennels. I said to him "I will see you there tomorrow", what time you need her for, he of course as many handlers started trying to put pressure on me, "you don't trust me, bla, bla, bla" and when that did not work, he started making fun of me "yes, my dog is a princess and doesn't travel with the other dogs in bus cargo", well I knew better, my gut was telling me this was not right so I let him bark.

Went home got my dad to buy me and airplane ticket an flew with my girl first thing in the morning the next day, my cousin picked me up and we made it to the Expocan safe. I spent the next three weeks in México City at Expocan keeping a close eye on my baby Fergie and her handler. Making sure she was treated right and putting up with the handler making fun of us. He nicknamed Fergie "pricipessa" and me the "pricipessa's mom". I said to him "you can bark as much as you want but my dog is not to go thru unnecessary stress, and the minute I see her not enjoying this, she is out and you are fired", yes I have always been quite direct and undiplomatic. LOL

On that trip he lost a dog, the dog actually died during transportation, it was a golden retriever puppy that never made it to the dog show and the handler didn't even tell the truth to the owners. He didn't even call them, he actually disposed of the dog body and ten days later when he came back and the owners went to get their dog, he said the dog passed of natural causes and they should talk to the breeder, when the dog actually arrived dead to México city after six hours in a crate in cargo, the dog probably suffocated.

Things like this happen all the time at dog shows, there is too much stress for the dogs. Fergie only showed a few times on a period of three years and then I retired her, during that period I also found her a better handler and she lived with me all the time. She only saw her handler for the dog shows never lived with them. She and I lived apart for a while when I was studying in Monterrey. She moved with me to Monterrey but she also lived with a lawyer/breeder friend of mine for a few months at his house in Mexico City, which actually saved her from being stolen or killed during an apartment break in I had while in Monterrey.

Fergie is an experienced traveler; she did travel a lot as a young show girl and also because she has moved with me quite often, to Monterrey, México City, back to Veracruz, to Ontario and now to Alberta. Not counting all the times she's been taken on road trips.

In 2007 she got certified as a therapy dog with the local organization and did that job for quite some time. Today she is 13 years old and enjoys being fully retired. She retired from the therapy dog group and travels with us to México for the holidays every year with her sister Peachy. Fergie enjoys perfect health and is still sporting a puppy clip which is a long coat. She loves being brushed, she comes to work with me every day, she is truly is a princess. She still sleeps in bed with us, and she always looks for the highest point in the bed or sofa to lay down. I believe she knows she is pretty, loves meeting people and other animals, sometimes this gets a little scary because she is sure every dog is her friend, and I always worry a little.

Fergie has this amazing interesting way to let us know what she wants, she would sit and stare at us, weather she wants water, food, go out or get lifted onto the bed she just will stare at you until you look at her. Then she tells you what she wants, she will point to her water dish, go the bedroom and put her paw on the bed, go to the door to be taken out and these are things no one trained her to do. She is also Peachy's teacher. She taught Peachy everything Peachy knows about being a dog. Even taught her to use her nose, taught her that is OK to get close to humans for treats and to be pet and lifted, how to ride in the car and many more things. Fergie truly adopted Peachy and looks after her all the time. Peachy looks for Fergie, as long as Fergie is around, Peachy feels safe. Fergie is now the pack leader when they are alone, Andrew clearly stepped down of the role a couple years ago when he completely lost his sight and Fergie took over. Animals are truly amazing.

Fergie loves getting her picture taken or even being on video; she is so used to it, because I'm always taking pictures of them, so they know to look at the camera. LOL.

Fergie is thirteen but she looks way younger and she behaves way younger too, she never had babies, in fact we spayed her almost a little too late, because she was a show dog she needed to be intact and we moved to Canada with her being intact, I was planning on showing her myself in Canada and add yet another championship to her resume of five championships and she is points away to be a world champion but anyway, I knew she had irregular cycles and one day I caught her liking herself too much. I do brushed her often and I also groom my own dogs, so while brushing her I discover she had a vaginal discharge and rushed her to the vet the next day to learn she needed to have emergency surgery. She had pyometra, which is the infection of the uterus, called also a silent killer because by the time the dog's exhibit signs of illness is, in most cases, too late, the uterus burst and infection spreads killing the dog. For her it was not too late, she was draining it by herself which was helping but she got fix that same day at the hospital. Since then she is being a happy healthy girl, we wish you eternal health and long life dear Fergie Girl!

Peachy

Well in the first part of the book you learned a lot about Peachy. She now is truly toothless, she lost her last two teeth a couple months ago, she is also thirteen years old and she is a toy poodle, a little apricot poodle girl, she now exhibits signs of happiness, especially when is feeding time and she is also bossy. She learned and developed her own ways to let us know what she wants. If she wants food she would run to us and then run to her dish so we know she wants to eat. She also does the shark dance at feeding time, imagine a shark going in circles around you, well now change the shark image with Peachy image running in circles around you, so you hurry up preparing her meal, and while she does that she keeps her mouth open and tongue hanging, as soon as you finish preparing her meal and she sees you lifting the dish from the kitchen counter she runs and stands by her crate. We hang their food dishes on their crate doors, they don't go inside the crates anymore they just stand outside and eat out of the hanging dish, this way they don't have to lower themselves too much, Peachy usually eats sitting.

Peachy is still not thrilled about grass. She would rather walk on concrete or patio stones. She also likes to do her business on concrete or stone rather than grass. She is still not fully house trained. In fact we think she is reversing her training, at some point she was letting us known when she wanted out but now she would pee anywhere and we are ok with it. We love her and accept her with all her limitations and challenges.

Peachy is still being seen occasionally by an animal communicator and she has overcome a few scares lately. In September 2011 we rushed her to emergency to learn she had pneumonia out of nowhere and the tricky part is she still won't show signs of illness. She doesn't show pain or anything. I did notice her behaving weird like putting her head up while sleeping the day before, but she was eating and drinking normally, so the next day she was still trying to keep her head up, still eating and drinking. When Ricardo picked her up and she fell asleep on his arms, well that was not normal so we rushed her to emergency to learn she needed to stay. The Doctor believed that was it, and the kind thing to do was to put her down, we decided to hospitalize her, after four days in the hospital she came home fully recovered. This year she had a root of one of her few teeth left infected which caused a nasal discharge, she was very low energy and I thought it was the end, we kept taking her to the vet and it did not seem to work, so it was time for an animal communication session. The communicator said Peachy was not ready to leave, she was just tired of being sick. With the help of the communicator we talked her into seeing a different vet, a holistic one, and it worked. She recovered, got strong and was able to get her two teeth left pulled out. She also got the root from the right canine pulled out, she still has a nasal discharge and she may have it for the rest of her life since the root caused a problem on the nose canal that creates the discharge.

Peachy also sees a rehab doctor because the years at the puppy mill caused her to have troubles with her legs. She is also thirteen years old but she looks much older, she has very little muscle, despite her good diet and good appetite, she of course has no teeth and also has problems with the left front leg. Her back legs are not strong either so we take her to laser acupuncture therapy and I give her energy healing sessions, this keeps her going, she loves her laser therapy, her most favorite part is the infrared heated pad she gets wrap into at the end of her laser sessions, she just falls asleep and smiles.

The other thing I believe keeps her going is her love for life and food. She is a little angel and no matter how bad of a day we had, coming home to these three seniors is always an adventure.

Another thing Peachy hates is being groomed and unfortunately she gets groomed a lot. She has no teeth she often gets food on her coat. She pees a lot and she sometimes gets pee on her fur too so we try to keep her as clean as we can without stressing her, but now she fight us, she is a little feisty fighter, we really love that she stands her grounds now, that is a sign of how much she has grown.

Peachy has also learned that people sitting at the dining table means food. So she will come running, wagging her tail and barking at us. We usually let her try what we eat, after all, we figure she does a lot coming all the way close to us to be ignored, once you lower a piece of food for her, she will jump and with all her strength close her gums on your fingers, she even closes her little eyes while she does this.

We are very proud of Peachy, she has come around and made a 180 degrees change, she went from the scared, fearful little football poodle girl to a feisty little girl, yes she is feisty now she will tell us what she doesn't like. Example when we bathe her, she would fight us, try to run away and screams at us, she is letting us know she hates baths but unfortunately she gets baths once a week or once every two weeks and we also wipe her face after she eats, she knows that as soon as she is done eating we will come with a wet warm towel, well we pick her up and she starts moving in our arms trying to get away, she doesn't like getting her face clean.

Peachy's favorite snack: Yogurt of any kind, she likes Greek, fruit, vanilla or plain.

Something Peachy never learned was to stretch, you know dogs will stretch their bodies when they get up or while sleeping, well Peachy doesn't know how to do it, neither has learned in seven years with us.

Tyra

At the time I was writing part II of this story, I really had no idea we were getting another dog, nor planned on doing so. How it happened... well I changed jobs and ended up working at a well-known grooming shop that belongs to a reputable and well known breeder. At the time I walked into the shop on June 15th 2013, I noticed there was a black poodle in a crate. The days passed and I started asking about the dog.

The girls that work at the shop said "oh that's Tyra, and she lives here", she lives here???. I said. Their answer was yes she lives here because if they (meaning the owners of the shop/ breeder) take her home, she barks and the neighbors complain, plus she doesn't like other dogs and Ana (to give a name to Tyra's previous owner) and her husband breed big dogs so Tyra can't live with them in the house, so that's why she is here.

To me this was totally unacceptable. This dog had been this person first show dog, and because she decided to get into breeding a more commercial breed, she had kept Tyra as a pet in a crate. Ana also had bred Tyra and of course sold the puppies. Tyra now was older and this woman could not breed her anymore so why keep her?.

I really know how common this is among dog breeders and knew that confronting this woman was not the way to go. Trying to make her understand why keeping a dog in a crate was wrong and why this poodle was, as they had labeled her, "neurotic" was not going to change Tyra's life.

I knew Tyra needed a new home, but I also knew we had three senior poodles that required our attention, Peachy was having leg problems and we were living in a hotel suite waiting for our house to be completed.

I talked to Ana who is really a very friendly and people oriented person and ask her what her plans were for Tyra. She said she was "looking" for a home for her but it was not easy because Tyra did not like other dogs, cried and barked all the time. She said Tyra was very attached to her and may not adapt to someone else. All I could think was, yes that's why she lives stuck in a crate, because she loves you. I said I could take her as soon as I moved into my house on July 15th; my plan was to really get Tyra out of that jail and find her a home.

The months went by and I was still living in the hotel suite. Because I was working at this place, I started to take Tyra out for pee breaks when I would arrive, at lunch time and when I left the place to go home. Tyra started recognizing me and liking me, but I was still sure I would have to find her a home, after all we had three dogs and Ricardo did not want a forth dog.

We finally moved into our house on August 16th and two days later we took Tyra home. Ana had told me that if I did not take her, she would put her down. She did not want to see Tyra anymore so I told Ricardo and we could not let that happen, so we ended up with four dogs.

To our surprise, we picked Tyra up on a Sunday evening; I went in the shop and got her. She jumped in the car like she had jumped in our car before and laid on the back sit, when we arrived home, she headed for the door and she got inside the house as if she knew she was home.

It took her about three days to realize she was free and no longer had to cry for attention or behave like a hysterical dog. She still wears her tail down must times, and still has sad eyes but she is now free, recovering from a long time ear infection and happy. She goes for walks everyday with Fergie, loves to be off leash and she's pretty obedient. She also jumps on our furniture like Fergie and Andrew, that's how she spends most of her days now.

She has a few belongings she had collected in her months with us, and old bed we gave her the day she arrived and three plush toys, she got two at a dog charity dinner party and the other one is a little pillow mom made for Peachy.

Tyra takes her toys out every time she goes out, and even though I never dreamt of getting another dog. I now believe Tyra came to us to make Peachy's departure easier on us and on Fergie.

Peachy "The Warrior Princess"

We don't know the exact day or year Tyra was born, because apparently she belonged to someone else before, so Ana did not have the information, or at least that is what she told us. Tyra was an unlucky dog like many show dogs out there, until she found us.

Diet

* *

Well I'm not a dietician, veterinarian or dog nutritionist but one thing I know for sure, natural diet is the best for my dogs and it's probably the best for us too. When we adopted Peachy we learned that she was being fed the raw diet. Well the rescuer said was the easiest and fastest way to get the rescues back to health. We, to be honest, were grossed out and it did not made any sense to give a raw chicken neck or a chicken wing to a tiny dog that had only five teeth left. Also I could only imagine Andrew and Fergie full of raw chicken blood and fat on their faces, fur and ears, the idea was gross. The rescuer also gave us a list of "holistic" dog food brands because she endured a lot from adopters refusing to feed their dogs raw chicken necks and backs.

At that time I was cooking for Andrew and Fergie this was after the big 2006/2007 dog food recall and after I learned that most dog food brands are manufactured and packaged at the same facility with different brands. I also learned that the dog food industry in the USA and Canada is not truly regulated. At the time of the dog food recall I was feeding my dog's top of the line poodle formula that is supposed to be specially formulated for poodles to keep them healthy and make them live a long happy life. When the dog food got recalled I promptly contacted the company that made the brand I was feeding my guys, and weeks later they emailed me back saying poodle formula was not tainted only the special diet formula for sick dogs was tainted with rat poison, so I emailed them back saying "can you assure me the poodle formula is safe" and their answer was "we cannot ensure anything" Wow!!. That totally opened my eyes. I have fed top of the line kibble to these dogs all their lives making sure I always bought the best brands only to learn they are all manufactured by the same company, that there is no quality standards and that they bring the ingredients from china with no previous analysis they throw it in to the mix that later becomes the kibble we feed our babies, our beloved pets, the members of our family.

I also learned that the meat they put in it is the meat that can't pass USDA food inspection for human consumption. Mostly meat that comes from the sickest animals result from industrial farming or the road kills or the animals that die during industrial farming transportation to the slaughter house, and not only that it made even more real the fact that in the news many pet owners were devastated by the loss of their pets caused by a rapid liver and kidney failure attributed to the rat poison in the dog food. The pet food shelves at the supermarkets where empty due to the recall and that was my turning point. When we picked up Peachy I was no longer a kibble feeder I was a dog cook, making sure my guys got enough lean protein and veggies of course cooked.

Adopting Peachy we learned that there were a few holistic brands and we decided to try buying holistic kibble but l did had two breeder friends that swore by the raw food diet and their dogs where never sick or had to visit the vet as often. So by January 2008 I researched the raw diet more and with the help and experience of my breeder friends I decided to switch the dogs to a raw diet. Andrew was having troubles with the Canadian winters and his arthritis was really bad, he was clearly in pain and the pain meds he was on seemed not to help him anymore so for him switching to raw was a life or death decision, within weeks Andrew was doing better, way more mobile and in less pain, was it possible that feeding him raw chicken, raw chicken bones and veggies was helping him so much. I have always given my dogs omega 3 fatty acids capsules, that was a trick I learned at the show rings, it helps with the coat, and I have also occasionally given them raw eggs and canned oil tuna since they were pups, again all for coat maintenance proposes, but this also helps their immune system.

I was thrilled by the result in my dogs, Andrew was pain free, Peachy and Fergie seemed to enjoy her meals more. Fergie especially because she was a picky eater, poodles can be picky about what they eat but Fergie would starve before eating boring kibble. We often had to mix hers with some wet food or chicken when I did not know better and I was a kibble feeder.

Today my dogs are old but super healthy and I attribute that to their diet. Again at some point I got disconnected because remember Charlie, well he was fed cooked chicken every day, wings and legs and necks and he was pretty healthy. All the other dogs in the house the working dogs, yes my dad bought kibble for them but it was usually mixed with left overs, like the remaining from lunch (in Mexico lunch is the biggest meal of the day, we often have soup and meat) so the dogs would and still get soup with some chicken wings and legs and whatever meat is left from lunch mix with their kibble at my parents' house.

I also remember as a kid when dad went on his hunting trips and packed everything in the truck, he packed the dog too but no kibble for the dog, the dog ate at hunting camp whatever they hunt, those dogs were happy to go on hunting trips, I remember them waiting to be loaded onto the truck with all the camping gear to make the long trip to the hunting spot.

My parents have a short hair German pointer that is 14 years old and likes to eat everything. He loves papaya at breakfast time, and my dad often gives him fruit at lunch time or gives him something of whatever snack dad is having. When dad is at the table Andrew, Fergie (when they lived in Mexico) and Sammy (a rescue poodle that lives in Mexico with my parents) were always next to him, because dad would share with them whatever he ate at lunch time or any time he sits at the table. Yes my dogs beg for food, and yes they are allowed to try anything we eat, in fact I believe is a lack of human manners eating in front of your dog and not sharing with him/her. LOL. In my experience the healthiest dogs are the ones that are allowed to try human food; they are not interested on getting into the garbage, or get poisoned or have to get rushed to the animal hospital because they got themselves into human food.

My dogs eat raw food mostly prepared at home so we can ensure that the ingredients are human grade, clean and organic. They also love snacks like cheese, chicken livers, liver treats, dehydrated chicken and fruits they are always ready to try fruit. They love mangoes, pears, bananas, apples, cherries, they are not so in love with veggies but they secretly eat them because we mix them with their raw chicken. There is still many veterinarians that don't approved of raw feeding your dog and there are still many myths about salmonella on dogs due to raw feeding but so far I have not yet seen a dog with salmonella or got salmonella from a dog. Today we have a good veterinarian that supports raw feeding and I believe in the future more vets will. Also my dogs don't smell bad because they eat raw, in fact they have no smell at all, is part of their breed they don't shed, they don't smell.

Another teaching from Peachy was eating right. Today I'm more aware of what I eat, and I'm no longer the crazy dieter I was. I am more into eating good proteins, good organic veggies and fruits, my husband still believes I'm a little crazy and just want to pay more for eggs when I buy my free range organic eggs, well he has not watched the FOOD INC documentary yet. When I did it was a huge eye opener. I also know about the illnesses caused by pesticides in our food since I did my thesis on it and at some point while working as an environmental consultant did a lot of research on chemicals and human exposure to them. As an animal lover well I just can't eat protein from an animal that had suffered at a farming mill that is not different than a puppy mill.

I'm still not a vegan or a vegetarian, because to be honest I don't love veggies as much but what I can do is to make sure the protein that I eat comes from animals that were treated decently, and in this matter I'm still educating myself. I do remember back in 2010 at an "I can do it" conference, I listened to Eldon Taylor who is a vegetarian and he said "since he became a vegetarian he is less prone to anger". He also talked about emotions on the animals and all the hormones released by the brain. How animals get killed inhumanly at the slaughter house and how he believes all those emotions get stuck in the meat we later eat. So it's something else to think about.

I recently stumbled in to a book called BEG by Lory Freeman and that book is an eye opener for all animal lovers. I have always refused to wear fur, in fact my first coat that had a mink collar I got it when one of my aunts passed away. I was probably twelve or thirteen but I was the only one that could fit in the coat so I got it. I asked my mother to remove the mink out of the coat. My mom believed I was crazy and she removed it but saved it in case later in life I changed my mind. Well guess what I have still not changed my position on that piece of mink. I don't want to wear it. And really when I was twelve or thirteen I had no internet neither I had a way to research about minks nor mink factories it just felt wrong.

So I'm not saying become a vegan or a vegetarian now because it's not an easy change and I'm not there yet nor I'm an expert on the matter, but what I'm trying to say is be more critical about your food, about what you put in your mouth, try as much as possible to get sustainable food sources, organic foods, cruelty free proteins, and try and feed your beloved pets less kibble and wet food and more human grade food.

I'm also not a fan of diet products, have never been because I don't know if you have noticed but they leave an after taste on your mouth and while doing my Masters I remember reading a paper about cancer, specifically breast cancer in younger girls and the link to diet products. My gut told me diet products where not good, my mouth confirm it, but the research truly opened my eyes and the little things I choose diet over regular that were mayonnaise and yogurt. I no longer do. It's better to eat the regular stuff but eat less, after all I eat mayonnaise very rarely and well yogurt now I eat the Greek, organic one and my dogs do too, we love Greek yogurt!

Zoos and Circuses

Well as an animal lover kid I did have different animals in the house like chickens, bunnies, birds, turtles, fish, a cat, a turkey and of course many dogs, growing up I did enjoy having many pets and today the only animal I believe can be a pet without being deprived of their animal life is a dog. Probably cats are good as pets too but I'm not a cat person.

Because I loved animals so much my parents loved taking me to the circus every time the circus was in town. I was little but I remember having the gut feeling that people hitting the animals to make them perform was not exactly right. Later in life I definitely asked my parents not to take me to the circus anymore. I could not stand seeing exotic animals reduced to a circus show for the pleasure of few people. Living in terrible conditions, in small cages and traveling all the time, often full of their waste because they did not have enough attention.

The Zoos causes me the same feeling, as well as the aquariums, I just can't believe animals that would mainly be happy living free in the wild can be happy in an enclosure for bigger that this enclosure can be. I can feel their sadness, and because we are a paradox, after we trained the animals and exploit them for circus, aquariums or zoo purposes when the animal turns around and kills the trainer, well we as humans freak out, kill the animal and make a big media thing about it but just think about it for a second. Imagine yourself forced to live in a small enclosure, a circus cage or an aquarium tank. Or like puppy mill dogs in small crates full of feces all your life or like show dogs that only get out of their crate to show, wouldn't you be neurotic? Wouldn't you attack your trainer?, I probably would, so next time you see a confined animal just look at their eyes and ask yourself, What do I feel right now?.

Pet stores

I love animals and there is nothing that enrages me more than pet stores carrying animals. I remember when I was living in Monterrey one pet store had a baby kangaroo for sale, but while it sold you could get your picture taken with the kangaroo, really?, later that week the baby kangaroo made the news, the local government authorities picked him up from the pet store because he had been illegally obtained in the black market from Australia. Honestly we need to start sabotaging this kind of pet stores, not only because they sell puppies that for sure come from puppy mills, but also because these animals are being mistreated.

As long as we buy our puppy at a pet store we are contributing to the problem. Next time you see a puppy at a pet store before buying it, please think of Peachy story and the many moms that are still producing these puppies while living in hell, because a puppy mill is very close to hell.

The horrors the mom of your beautiful pet store puppy is enduring so you can buy a puppy at a pet store. Puppy that must likely will be ill, have some behavioral issues or die due to their rough start in life. These pups are often taken from their moms too early because there is no room in the puppy mill cage for them, and these cages are most times packed with feces so pups can get sick easily also the smaller they are the faster they will sell at the pet store, the faster you will fall in love with them but before buying this adorable pet store puppy do your homework, Please!!.

If you are already in the pet store and have been trapped by the adorable puppy face looking at you from that horrible glass pet store enclosure, before holding the pup in your arms or even while holding it, do me a favor, and honor Peachy's and many puppy mills dogs life's by asking to be helped by a supervisor, once you have the supervisor ask simple questions like:

1. I would like to get this puppy but before I buy it I would like to know what kind of guarantee the store has on them?
2. Do you know where the puppies come from?
3. Do you have paperwork that could ensure me that I'm getting a healthy well bred puppy?
4. Can you ensure me that the puppy doesn't come from a puppy mill? If there answer is yes they are probably lying to you ask them for the paperwork. If the puppy comes from a good breeder they will have the name of the breeder and his information, to say the least, as well as puppy's first vaccinations, name of puppy's parents and more info on the generals of the puppy.

Ask them for proof of vaccinations. Any good breeder vaccinates their puppies at least with the first puppy shot before selling them.

5. Have you seen the place where the puppies were born? Or did you get the puppies delivered by a broker? If they can assure you the puppies parents are pure breed yorkies, poms, poodles, labra doodles (even though this is not a pure breed but the poodle mixes are very popular these days, and they are marketed as pure breed hypoallergenic dogs, lie). They must be able to answer, after all; you are paying a good amount of money for the pup. The least they can do is have the right paperwork, do their research, give you answers but they won't.

In a recent trip to a mall that prides itself of being the largest mall in north America I found myself wondering in to the pet store who sells not only puppies but also exotic birds, I asked to talked to the person in charge of the puppies as if I wanted to buy one of them. Well the person in charge, puppy manager or whatever they called her, had no way to answer my questions, you know why because they buy these puppies for cheap from the middle man that buys it from the puppy millers and later sells them to the pet store owner, they probably do the same with their exotic birds, but instead of getting them from a puppy mill they get them in the black market so they can get them for cheap, turn around and made top dollar on them.

So you walked into the pet store by the beautiful yorkiepoo, cockapoo, labra doodle, beagle, cavalier, poodle, fox terrier, papillon or whatever your favorite puppy because you fell in love with it, felt sorry for it because it was sitting in the glass enclosure at the pet store, so you get your credit card buy the pup no questions asked. It was a total emotional buy, you did not think about how the pup got to the pet store, the mom of the pup suffering at the puppy mill living in hell so you can have your puppy, you didn't even ask for papers for the pup, or vaccinations nothing, if you are lucky you go home with a new pup and a whole bunch of puppy stuff to train your puppy, weeks later your puppy dies, because it was a sick puppy product of being born in a puppy mill, you are devastated, heartbroken, inconsolable, you are a victim, you tell all your friends how horrible your puppy experience was and how traumatized you are or your kids are, and you spent over a thousand dollars on a pet store puppy. Well sorry to burst your bubble but the only victim here is the mom of that pup that is still at the mill.

Well here is a thought that may just work for you, if you are going to spend a thousand dollars buying a puppy because it's the dog you want, and you can't get it from a rescue or at least you believe you can't adopt it, well smarten up and find a breeder. A good breeder who at least will make you see the parents of your puppy, show you the conditions where your puppy was born, give you papers because for that amount of money you can get a pure breed dog from a breeder with papers and a replacement guarantee. So if you are definitely shopping for a pup do your due diligence, spend your money wisely and don't support pet stores, because in doing so you are supporting puppy mills, puppy millers, middle mans, back yard breeders and a whole bunch of people that are making money out of the pain of a living animal, you are contributing to the torture of an innocent soul and to a huge problem.

There is a book called "Saving Gracie" that is the story of another puppy mill survivor just like Peachy and the efforts of ASPCA to close down the puppy mill where Gracie and hundreds of other dogs lived a life of misery and horror, I strongly recommend you to pick it up and read it.

Oh and by the way I left the mall pet store after talking to the puppy manager and expressing to her how I felt, I said "I would never buy a puppy from you, because these dogs come from puppy mills and I can't believe you guys are doing this", I know the puppy manager is just a kid trying to get by with a job, but maybe something clicks in her and she realizes selling puppies without having any info is not right and maybe she raises her voice to her boss, maybe she awakens and becomes an animal advocate. You just never know, I was not rude to her or emotional, I was calm and raised my point calmly, my whole thing was not to beat the poor girl down nor to buy a pup or start a revolution right there and then, but to maybe make something click in her brain and awaken her.

By the way every time I'm at a mall or shopping and find a pet store, I go in mainly to see what I can get for my pooches, but if the store has puppies or exotic animals I ask for the manager and question them to this day I have not yet found a pet store manager that is able to pull paperwork to ensure me his puppies or the exotic animals he/she sells in the store come from good breeders or are legally caught in the wild so just think about it.

FACT: *Good breeders don't give their dogs to pet stores.*

Finding a good breeder

Well this book is not about buying dogs, it's about stopping puppy mills and get more people to rescue dogs but since I'm guilty of having three pure breed poodles that are show dogs (retired now) and I have been in the dog show circles, I believe I can help you with some tips of what I have seen at the dog shows and what I consider a good breeder.

At dog shows there are people from all walks of life, many of them are breeders, lots of them are handlers, groomers, trainers. Now here comes the tricky part, finding one that has a breeding license, is recognized by the AKC, FCI, FCM, CKC or whatever your national kennel club organization is called, and also has not been charged with animal cruelty, but how do we do this?, because remember the guy that was Gracie's breeder (from the book saving Gracie) was in the 70's and 80's a world recognized handler, so when he started breeding, he had made a name for himself, people believed they were getting good, cruelty free bred, pure breed dogs, but the reality was, this man ran one of the worse and largest puppy mills in the United States.

If you really want a pure breed certified dog, a dog with pedigree, I want to believe is because you are passionate about dog shows and want to show a dog, otherwise I find no reason for buying a pure breed, because you may as well find your pure breed at your local shelter or at a pure breed specific rescue. Or maybe just by walking into your new work place, like I found Tyra.

But let's say the case is you want to be the next personality in the dog show rings and perhaps in the future become a good breeder so that's your reason to get a dog from a breeder, well let's do some homework.

Before going in a pure breed shopping spree, research the breed you want to get, read as many books on the breed as you can, get familiar with the breed and ask yourself, am I really the type of person who can have a poodle and provide for it not only financially, but mentally, have the time to brush my dog every day, take the dog for walks, stimulate her/his brilliant poodle mind, pay for monthly trips to the groomers, train my dog so it not a classic poodle stereotype (a yappy dog) but what the breed was meant to be. A smart, faithful, people lover, loyal companion, brush his/her teeth every day; I'm in a position to care for this dog for the next eighteen or twenty years of my life because some dogs have a very long life span. Remember my Andrew is fifteen years old and going strong. Now I use a poodle example because that's what I have had as a companion for the past 25+ years so I know the breed and quite honestly love the breed, plus the subject of this story is Peachy who is a poodle too; but in reality you should ask these questions any time you see the newest dog movie and you feel like running to get yourself a Golden Retriever, Dalmatian, Beagle or whatever breed the movie star was or any time you are sitting watching TV and you see the advertisement for toilet paper with a cute Labrador and feel like rushing out to get one, well these breeds are very active and if you are a couch potato, chances are you probably not a good match for any of the doggie stars or the toilet paper pooch,(chances are you are buying yourself a problem that later will be dumped at a local shelter to be killed with the other millions of pure breeds and mutts that are killed every year at shelters because people don't do their homework, don't research and only buy because they can.

Well let's stop that. So if you don't want to immerse yourself into reading breed books, find out when the next dog show in your area is, go there and find the dog you want, if you are lucky enough chances are the dog will be shown by the breeder, so you can talk to the breeder and start asking questions about the breed.

A good breeder loves to educate people about their dog breed. A good breeder is proud of their dogs, treats the dogs well, travels with his/her dogs to dog show, handles his/her dogs by themselves (meaning very rarely they send dogs to shows with handlers), does not debark the dogs (debarking is a common practice that some breeder use where the dogs get their vocal cords cut so the dogs can bark, often done because in a breeding facility most likely you will find up to ten dogs or more, so commercial breeders who don't care for the animals wellbeing debark for the human comfort).

A good breeder is often a professional who has a job for which they live out of and they love dogs so much, love dog shows, know so much about their breed that decide to start breeding but during the week they are often doctors, lawyers, accountants, engineers, veterinarians, dog groomer, business owners who love dogs, wanting to preserve a breed, start breeding them, often their dogs live inside the house, run free in the house, and are well taken care of. This kind of people will be the ones that at a dog show will love to talk to you about their dogs, their breeds. Because they pride themselves on their expertise, and often they will be busy at the show grooming and paying attention at what is going on in the show ring but if they can't take care of you at the moment, they will ask you to come back later or give you a business card so you can keep in touch with them.

If you find yourself at a dog show talking to a so called breeder that is more a sales person, trying to push his breed or worse a puppy they brought to the show for sale, well that's is clearly a red flag!, also if the breeder doesn't want you to see the breeding facility, or refuses to show you the parents of your potential puppy, red flags!; You may be encountering a puppy miller, back yard breeder or someone that calls itself a show breeder but has clearly no idea of what he/she is doing, is only in the breeding business to make money and does not care about the well-being of the dogs.

A good breeder will also question you, they often ask you Why do you want that specific kind of dog?, What do you know about the breed?, If you have ever had a let's say Poodle before?, What have been your past experiences as a dog owner?, What has happened to your previous dogs?, if you have had dogs before?, What kind of house do you have?, Who do you live with? What are your plans for the dog? What will be the dog accommodations?, What do you do for a living?, and many more questions, I like to see it as if they are placing one of their kids into an adopting home so don't feel discouraged or intimidated because they are interrogating you, If you are being interrogated by the breeder, you must likely have found yourself a good breeder.

A good breeder will often invite you to his house/ breeding facility so you see how the dogs live, and how the parents of your future pup live and are treated. You may end up visiting the breeder's house more than one time. They also like to create relationships with the people that buy dogs from them and this is because they like to make sure and occasionally check on the dogs they sell.

When I bump into any of my two breeders the first question they asked me, how is Andrew or Fergie doing?, and they will always close the conversation with "if you have any questions, don't hesitate to call me" and "please don't be an stranger, drop me a note every once in a while so I know how Andrew or Fergie are doing", to this day fifteen and thirteen years after I purchase my guys I'm still in touch with their breeders.

A good breeder will also make you sign an agreement saying that if you for any reason don't want the dog anymore, you are obligated to bring the dog back to the breeder at any stage of the dog's life, the breeder is obligated to take the dog back no questions asked and find the dog a new loving home.

A good breeder will never, and I emphasize never advertise puppies for sale in the local newspaper or the internet listing; you know Craig list, Angies list, kijijiji, Mercado Libre, ebay or whatever the case will be. These ads are often signs you will be dealing with a bad breeder, a back yard breeder, a puppy miller, etc. The breeders that I like are the ones that in order for them to have a litter of pups, they have a home for each pup in the litter, a home they have researched and approved as a forever loving home, these breeders often have a waiting list, and you may find a breeder that tells you, well I don't have puppies until next year or I have pups but they are all sold, you may want to put your name on their waiting list because they are totally doing the right thing, not only breeding dogs for the sake of making money.

Good breeders often have a small margin of profit on the dogs they breed, because by the time the pup goes home, they have been vaccinated, checked by the veterinarian, checked for common pure breed issues like bad eyes, bad knees, bad elbows, and bad hips that are common on some pure breed dogs. Yes because in order to create a perfect conformation dog, breeders have been playing God by doing genetic selections for generations that sometimes only messes up what the breed was naturally intended to be, so now some breeds need to be eyes, hips, knees certified to ensure you, the buyer, that the dog you are getting is a healthy dog free of expensive veterinarian care in the future. Some of these breeders even do temperament testing so by the time you pay close to a thousand dollars, (same money that you will pay at the pet store for a puppy mill dog that doesn't have any of this care, nor was born in a healthy environment), a big portion of that money, the breeder uses to pay for all the checkups and testing they do to give you a healthy pure breed show quality dog, or pet quality pure breed, because not all the dogs that are born from champion dogs are necessarily show material, some of them are and can only be pure breed expensive, healthy and well bred pets. A good breeder knows this and will be happy to sell you one of this pet quality pure breed at a lower price.

Again this book is really not to give you the guidelines and send you out finding your ideal dog and purchasing it from a breeder, but I can't tell you that all the breeders in the world suck and that you should only adopt dogs, like many people do, even though I'm pro adoption, and totally against buying at pet stores. I'm also a firm believer that knowledge is power and that is what this second half of the book is all about. I have to be fair to what I know; I know not all breeders are cruel monsters and in fact as much as I disagree with still breeding dogs, I do have good friends that are good breeders, who do the right thing for their dogs, who have tons of knowledge on their breeds, who received dogs back after ten, twelve, fourteen years of being sold. Because the people that bought the dog divorced or the dog is old and they don't want to deal with it, and my breeder friends get the dog back no questions ask, go above and beyond to find the dog a loving home where he/she can spend the rest of their lives. So I do know people that breed dogs because they love them, not to make money out of the dogs and I know there are still many breeders like the ones I'm friends with, you just need to do your homework, and find them.

Also you don't necessarily have to buy a dog from a good breeder, they often have dogs that are retired from dog shows or breeding, and not necessarily are old dogs. A show dog retires pretty early in their life; they often retire at four to six years old or younger. Often they get bred once or twice during that period, good breeders will spay or neuter the dog and find a good home for the dog where the dog can spend the rest of his/her life as a pet. The breeders place them usually in family environments because they often have up to ten dogs in their house that they are working with (more than ten dogs for a single person is just too hard to take good care off, so that's why they will not keep more than that as breeding stock), meaning grooming them, going to dog shows with them, training them and keeping a retired dog is often no fair for the dog, these dogs are used to having lots of attention, they are brushed every day, groomed at least once a week to preserve the coat, travel every weekend and once they retired well the attention the breeder will give them is not the same. The dog will no longer travel to dog shows, therefore the dog gets often shaved down on kennel cuts. You can provide for the retire show dog in your home way more attention as your loving pet, as a member of your family so that's why many breeders place their retired dogs in loving homes, I can assure you a good breeder does this with a heavy heart but knows is the best for the retired dog, to go and live life as a beloved pet.

So knowing all this once you find a good breeder, you can always ask if they have any retired dog for adoption, do the math, is a win win for you, because you are getting the pure breed dog you want, a dog with pedigree, a retired show dog that is not too old and is fully trained, knows how to travel so you can take your new member of the family everywhere with you, knows how to behave, is house broken, cage trained, has been fixed. Open your mind to this possibility because even if you get an older retired dog, you are winning. Some breeders may ask you to cover the spay/neuter fee and that is also fair, after all, you are getting a well-trained, healthy, well balanced retired pure breed that you wanted for a portion of a what you would have pay at a pet store getting a sick puppy and contributing to the problem or even for free.

Finding a trainer

This matter I learned it the hard way, you see even though I was born a dog lover and had been always involved with dogs, well the first time I got introduce to dog obedience training, was by the local kennel club in my home town. I'm Mexican, and in my home town Veracruz the local kennel club which I joined at age eighteen, only admitted people with pedigree dogs that wanted to compete. At the time they were not focused on helping regular dog owner learn how to train their non-pedigree dog. So even though I had tried to join earlier, I did not have a dog with papers (that's how pedigree dogs are often refer as). I only had pets so I was not welcome with the kennel club people. It has been brought to my attention that since then, that has change and they accept people with mutts that only want to train their dog for obedience and be able to walk their dog without being dragged. As I was so curious about learning how to train a dog, I got Andrew. Sadly the training method I learned at that time, fifteen years ago, was not the best and is a method that I no longer use, but to my surprise this training method is still used by many kennel clubs in North America.

    The main trainer was a member of the club who was also a military doctor and he was a very strict guy. Therefore his training methods where not necessarily the more positive ones or the best ones for the dogs. He based his method on making the dog respect you at all cost, so not necessarily hitting the dog but we were forced to have our dogs in chocker collar and six feet leather leashes at all times. The dogs needed to be under control at all times. This chocker collar method that is still used by some kennel clubs now a days, is based on choking your dog until they will learn to obey, in other words, you are taking the spirit out of your dog, forcing the dog to be submissive and terrified of punishment. Well I was not the most successful trainer in the club because I allowed Andrew to get away with murder, he was not punished (choke) as the other dogs in the club, when I was yelled to correct my dog, I did pull on his leash to close his chocker, but I never pulled to choke him or hang him because he disobeyed like many of the club members did. Yes you read it well, hanging the dog by the neck by pulling up on the collar and lifting the dog from the floor. It is a common practice in this obedience training method used specially with bigger dogs.

I found hanging the dog by the neck brutal and I still do. But the club interest was to create perfect dogs for competitions. My objective was to be able to teach my dog sit, stay, come and perhaps walk off leash without putting him at a risk of being ran over by a car or attacked by other dog. So I did mainly what I wanted, plus Andrew really is a ten pound poodle that when he gets "aggressive to other dogs or people" I just pick him up, and if is the case, put him in his crate so he can cool down; it got to the point that I didn't even have to pick him up, I used to say "Andrew crate" or "Andrew enough" and he knew it was time to settle, he still obeys "Andrew enough" now that he's blind he sometimes growls at nothing and when he hears his command, he knows he can settle and not worry about anything, there is nothing to growl to.

Andrew was a character at the local kennel club, because he walked into the training facility as he owned the place. He was all proud and would not allow other dogs to get close to me. This was frowned upon by the main trainer, but because I had Andrew under control, he would not kick us out of the club. But he never liked Andrew. I have to admit Andrew was an Alfa male and very protective of his pack, (he considered me part of his pack). He used to guard my doors at my parents' house. Yes is hilarious having a ten pound poodle guarding the bathroom door while you shower, but he felt that was his job and I just let him be. He did mean business while guarding the doors so really no one messed up with him.

Then my father got Pinto the short Hair German Pointer. Pinto came to us as a gift, his mom, a retired show dog, was given away by her former owner to a "good home" without being fixed (huge mistake), and the new owner knowing she had papers and was a show champion decided to make money out of her by keeping her in the patio and getting her to have pups as many occasions as he could trick someone with a pure breed show male to breed with him.

Pinto was born in the middle of winter in a patio with no protection from the elements. His loving mom did her best to keep Pinto and his siblings dry and warm. My home town gets really humid, rainy and windy during the winter. All Pinto's mom could find was an abandoned run down old boat in the open patio and she kept the pups there. The pups often got wet and Pinto being the runt of the litter got sick. The so called breeder who knew my dad, and learned that dad wanted another pointer decided to give Pinto to us.

By the time we got Pinto he was an eight week very ill puppy, I remember going with dad to this so called breeder house to pick a puppy. And well the man pretty much received us in the patio we got to see the mom and all the pups but he quickly picked Pinto up and gave it to us. He said "this is the puppy I reserved for you". This man knew Pinto was sick and he believed Pinto would die in a couple of days but he did not say anything to us. I got the puppy in my arms; hop back on dads' truck and off we went to buy the dog food.

This "breeder" told us Pinto was eating. It was all a Lie, Pinto did nothing but to shake in my arms all the way home, when we got home, I gave him some food and water, Pinto would not eat, in fact he keep shivering and did not want to move much, very unusual for a Pointer puppy. I convinced my father to call the veterinarian, of course it was a Sunday evening, and we chased a vet down in the city to get Pinto medical attention. Pinto survived, but he really spent three days in misery being seen by the Sunday vet that really was not prepared for a case like Pinto's.

Seeing a sick puppy it's the worse thing ever. I remember Pinto would not be able to control his legs and stand for long, he would shiver and by the time we found him a new Vet, he had puke a few times and had convulsions. He was also not eating. The new Vet, a wonderful medicine woman, was brutally honest with us telling us that Pinto was very ill with pneumonia due to being born and lived in the cold patio. Pinto also had ulcers in his throat, she said Pinto probably ingested water with some chemical at the house he was born and he was very congested having only half lung to breath with, she said it did not look good. Pinto had to stay in the hospital and we could be called in a couple days. She did not expect Pinto to recover, but she was going to do her best. She also said that if Pinto recovered, he was not going to be a normal dog, due to high fever he could end up being deaf, blind, or stupid. Well miraculously Pinto Recover and he's fourteen years old today.

Because I'm only five feet one inches tall and I was less than 100 pounds at the time, for me was a necessity to teach Pinto basic obedience and not be dragged by him while walking him. I started bringing him to the kennel club, but I just could not control Pinto at all, my boyfriend at the time started helping me and Pinto dragged him down the training facility several times, so we decided to find him a trainer. At the club there were members that where already certified trainers and we chose a younger guy thinking he may be gentler with Pinto.

Well we were absolutely wrong, and here it comes... observe your dog behavior in front of other people especially if this person is your dog's trainer/ dog walker, Pinto should had been excited to see the Trainer/walker because that meant going out on a long fun walk, but instead we started to notice that Pinto would not want anything to do with this guy, we talked to the guy and he said well is normal, bla, bla, bla. Today I know better, if your dog wants nothing to do with a human beware, there is something in behind.

One day I decided to go and see Pinto's training progress, I went with a friend to see Pinto. While training to my surprise, Pinto broke a sit/stay, and the so called trainer went to catch him and kick Pinto in between the back legs. Not only that, this "trainer" used to wear steel toes boots that is also a common practice among rude trainers. So watch how your trainer dresses, (steel toe boots are a giveaway that the trainer likes to kick dogs and hit them). Anyhow going back to the moment, this man had the nerve to kick my poor

Pinto in front of us. I went crazy, I'm very short fused and I with all my 100 pounds and small body, started yelling at this man to stop, unbelievably it took him some time to stop, he did not stop right away. I went up to him asked him to get away from my dog and fired him right in the spot not only that, I threaten to expose him, and I did, I was infuriated and I made sure this guy would not put his hands on any other dog ever, as a result he stopped training dogs because people started realizing what he was doing to the animals.

Pinto though had permanent damage, emotional and physical damage, Pinto ended up having testicular surgery because when Pinto was being trained he was not fixed yet, and he also had prostate surgery, Pinto developed a testicular tumor and bleeding from the prostate, I do believe all the kicking the so called trainer did to Pinto had something to do with this. Also Pinto does not like going for walks, he is extremely nervous during walks, if he hears a loud noise he will try to hide, dragging whoever is walking with him.

So if you happen to choose a trainer or dog walker for your dog, do yourself and your dog a favor and read your dog body language when the trainer/walker comes near your dog. Also check your dog for painful spots, bruces in his/her back legs after training and walking with a third party. Especially inside the legs, trainers like to kick inside because if they get carry away the dog owner is less likely to notice bruces or a bump inside the dog's leg. Pinto also would not let anyone touch his back legs; he's terrified; all I can say is I should have been more tuned into him and more alert. I should never left Pinto alone with the trainer, but this was my learning, and now I'm passing it to you so it does not happen to your beloved pet.

Veterinarians

I'm very inclined to work with veterinarians that are into rescue and will volunteer their work to help animals or help people that rescue animals. In Mexico was easy for me to find a veterinarian that was into veterinary medicine for the love of dogs more than to only make money. In fact all the veterinarians that I know in México either volunteer their work for shelters, run their own spay and neutering campaigns in remote areas of México, or help the people that rescue dogs with services and by advertising the dogs for adoption.

But when I moved to Canada I first lived in a small border city, in northern Ontario, right in the border with the USA (Michigan) and honestly, I'm very thankful for that, because in this little Canadian town Vets are so disconnected. it seems to me they had forgotten why they became veterinarians, they are in for the money and nothing else, it took me a few months of going around in this small town and try to find a vet that I could work with, that I could bring my dogs to without trying to be scammed every time I came in, and sadly I could not find one, I ended up crossing the border and finding an American veterinary clinic that was more into helping the animals. In fact the place that my dogs ended up being clients for the past six years in the USA, is a clinic that helps the Canadian rescue group with spaying/neutering and veterinary care at low cost, they also help the local shelter so I was totally ok bringing my dogs there.

My point here is, be critical, because I found in this particular small Canadian town the vets like to sell you unnecessary testing for your dog. A simple routine checkup ends up becoming a thousand dollar bill. I found some vets like to play with people emotions, but as dog owners we need to be critical, use our mind and not let our love for our pooches blind us. If you have a gut feeling that your dog does not need extra testing like unnecessary blood work, diagnostic imagine when you only took it for a routinely yearly vaccination checkup, must likely your dog doesn't need it. If your pooch, eats, drinks, is happy, active and releases itself well, you just took it to the Vet because it needs vaccinations and all of the sudden the vet believes your dog might be at risk of "X, Y or Z" but for that the Vet needs to do further testing, well you may have found a Vet that is in for the money and it won't hurt you to look for a new Veterinarian.

There are still plenty Veterinarians that are in for the love of animals, those that help shelters and rescues, those that own mutts and special needs dogs, and honestly it feels good to support a veterinary clinic that gives back. So find yourself a good, well-grounded and connected veterinary clinic, one that you know you can trust, that you know helps the community, that will help you too if you ever find yourself in need of help.

I now live in Alberta and I have found my guys excellent veterinarians, super connected people, which rescue dogs, give back and feed raw to their beloved mutts and for that I'm extremely grateful.

How can you help?

Well I'm a firm believer in volunteering. Volunteering will help you learn, will connect you with other people, and will help the animals, or whatever soul you choose to help by volunteering. I really believe that if kids, teens, young adults and adults would focus their spare time volunteering we will have a better world, not so chaotic. Volunteering helps us become better as humans, opens our heart and quite honestly keeps young people out of trouble.

Just think about it if the Boston Marathon bombers would have had instead involved themselves walking dogs at the local shelter or volunteer for a soup kitchen or any other organization, they would have had no time to think about bombing and injuring a whole bunch of innocent people.

In my case volunteering has help me connect with people that cares about animals, especially dogs, and when you start caring for such an innocent soul, like an animal soul, then you start seeing the world different. You feel the need to help when natural disaster strike, I do believe volunteering helps us in many ways to become more human and more humane.

When I said volunteering you don't necessarily have to run to your local shelter and help walking dogs or cleaning dog runs, or cleaning the other creatures. There are so many other programs that you can get involved with like helping organizing fund raises, or helping spread the word, or reclutting volunteers.

What about organizing your own fund raising to help a charity, or even to help your neighbor. You can organize, raffles, events, bake sales, lemonade sales or better ask people that for your birthday instead of giving you a gift to give a donation to the charity of their choice.

You can also foster an animal on death row, or take your clothes that you no longer like/use or haven't been able to wear for a while and bring them to a local people shelter, or clean your towels and blankets cabinet and donate what you don't like, need or want to the local animal shelter. There are many ways you can help when I say volunteering I don't necessarily expect each and every one of you to go out and give your time to a charity, but to try to do something that may require you little to no effort and will make another soul happy, will make a difference in your community.

I've been volunteering my time to dog rescue organizations for many years and is something that doesn't cost me a dime. And honestly I have got back way more of what I have given, I have met wonderful people to whom I have become friends with, it has made my moves to different cities easier, and I have had lots of fun. I can tell you that today I know many people around the world thanks to having been able to give a little of my time and volunteered in an organization. In my case has always been related to animals because that's what I'm passionate about, that's what makes my soul happy and my heart sings.

Donating money is another thing you can do, often we believe we are on a tight budget and we cannot spare a dime, but money is only energy and the more you give, the more it comes back to you, at this time I'm not close to an opulent situation, neither I'm close to the life style I was raised into, I was very fortunate and even though I was born and raised in México, I never lacked anything. In fact, today I can see I had abundance of things, perhaps a little too much. At this point sometimes I also worried about my budget but I still donate a little money every month to support animal causes. I like to think of it as the money that otherwise would had been lost in the laundry or wasted in something I don't need, instead is doing something for another living soul. And the whole intention of this book well as I stated it in the beginning is part of my efforts to raise money and help stop puppy mills.

Imagine for a second if every single company and product that exist out in the market would donate a portion of their profits to the charity of their choice. Well we would have less issues and a better world, we would be living in harmony.

As an environmentalist for me is very hard not to be an activist because I have seen that thru my activist work, my volunteering work, my dog rescue work, I have influenced the people around me, and I even have been able to change the minds of many friends. In fact many of my friends have adopted pure breed dogs from rescues and every so often when they need a dog or know of someone that wants a dog I get a request to find a specific breed, of specific age and specific characteristic, to this day I'm proud to report I have find that specific dogs in rescues.

I'm not a Saint or want you to be one, I just want to inspire you to give a little, let you know it takes no effort, no sacrifice and it pays back a million times. In case you want to try. As they say the energy you put out is the same energy that comes back to you.

Also I like to believe that when my time on earth is up, I'll have many dogs waiting for me on the other side.

Adults, seniors and special dogs

Well to this day I still see at shelters and rescues that adults, seniors and special needs dogs like blind or deaf dogs get passed by, in fact on my most recent visit to our local shelter, I found a eleven year old sharpei that is blind who happened to be for adoption, at a special adoption fee of fifty dollars and still no one had adopted her.

We as humans have this all wrong. Dogs that are "handicap" are way more able than people with the same disability, dogs use their noses first so for them to be blind means nothing, they also have the incredibly ability to memorize your house lay out. So very rarely they will bump into something. In fact as a mom of a special needs dog, I can tell you that you won't be able to tell Andrew is blind until you get to see his eyes, he is very independent and moves around just fine. To be honest yesterday at the shelter I was a little upset to see the sharpei and a couple other blind dogs that for sure had a home, and because they were blind adults or seniors now their owners had the brilliant idea to dump them at the shelter. Knowing their adoption chances are very slim to none, not to mention my husband who is not a fan of going to shelters with me, he was boiling when he saw the blind old dogs in the shelter, he turned to me and said "I can't believe it, how can they do something like that, it will be like us bringing Andrew to the shelter because he's blind and old, we'll never do that", and I said you got it right, indeed we will never do that.

But the things that you should know are:

- Adult dogs are way easier to train than puppies, especially when they have been homeless or in shelters after their family dump them because they are old, these dogs really appreciate second chances. Will do anything to please you, are quieter, won't chew your stuff or be crazy like a puppy. They will love you unconditionally and be grateful that you

gave them a spot in your house and in your heart to enjoy their golden years. Some of them will still have up to ten years to love you and remind you every day how much they care about you.
- Senior dogs, well is not fair because dogs by the age of eight or ten years old are already considered senior, and our human misconception of a senior is a sick, run down, not fun. But I dare you to see it differently, senior dogs are dogs with a lot of wisdom, they had lived their lives probably as someone pet and then betrayed and abandoned at the shelter. They will love you to death for giving them a second chance, will need fewer walks, and will remain on what I call a meditative state while you are at work, or what the world see as a dog that sleeps while they work. So when you come home, these wonderful lovable seniors are ready to have dinner, go for a short or long walk depending on their day preferences and then cuddle with you watching TV or why not sleeping with you. Don't let the age foul you because some dogs live longer than people expect them. Don't stereotype, not because they are older, they are necessary sick, think of your grandfather, many grandparents are still very active this days.
- Adult dogs and senior dogs are perfect for families that have no time to train a puppy and desperately want a dog.
- Seniors for seniors, well this is wonderful is an idea I saw on the internet that many shelter are pairing senior owners with senior dogs, and well all I can tell you is I would not like my parents to get a puppy, I rather have them get a senior dog because it will be more in tune with their life style, plus they won't have the risk of been dragged and injured by a puppy.
- Special needs dogs are not for everyone, but if you are up for the challenge I think you will find yourself very surprised and amazed by the experience. I like to see special needs dogs as warriors and great teachers because they don't live dueling on what they can't do; they just live life as a

non-handicapped dog, that is a teaching. They learn to live with their disability and be happy about it, not grouchy. Another big teaching. Many of these dogs are disabled due to being abused by a human and they will still trust humans. They will still love you for giving them the opportunity of being part of your life; they will still do their best to be a normal dog and not disappoint you. How can you say no to them? How can you think about disposing of a dog because its back legs don't work or because is blind or deft, because he/she has a lifetime illness.

- So please next time you are looking for a pet, don't pass by the old ones or the special ones, go into the shelter or into the search engine with an open mind and a wide open heart, you never know what you will find, and perhaps the old or special dog that you think you are rescuing, ends up rescuing you and lecturing you. Be open to the possibilities and let life surprise you!.

Part III

Sharing our family Pictures

Introduction

I started this book project over a year ago, in the summer of 2012. I knew for many years (over ten Years), I needed to write a doggie story about one of my rescues, and that the story needed to be a kids book, well it was not until last summer that the story took form and this summer I finally took the steps to find a publisher and add part II, life has caught up with me this year, with our move to Alberta and not having a house, closing my business to be able to move, and trying to publish my book.

But three weeks ago on September 27, 2013, Peachy left us and that changed my priorities in life. During the first week after her passing I quit my job to dedicate time to finish her book and then part III came to life.

So from our hearts to yours, I hope you enjoy it.

Peachy's last teaching to me is "focus on what is important in life, on what makes your heart sing".

Writing about her makes my heart sing and has helped me in my grieving process.

We love you Peachy girl!!!.

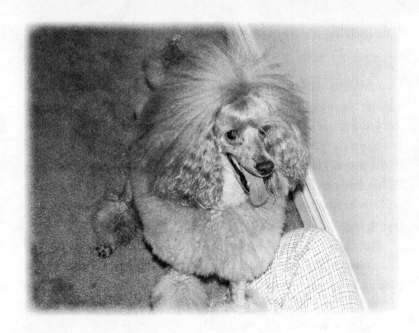

Fergie May 2006

This is one of Fergie's first Pictures in Canada when we just moved, you can tell she is a gentle soul and she was always up for the fun, she is a miniature Poodle about ten pounds with her beautiful red color.

May 2006 Fergie and Andrew playing

When we (meaning Andrew, Fergie and me) first moved to Canada in May of 2006 after marring Ricardo, we used to live in a basement apartment we rented in this little town called sault Ste. Marie Ontario. In the picture you can see Fergie and Andrew waiting for me to throw the toy at them so they can run up and down the hall way and get the toy back to me, we used to do this a lot since Sault Ste. Marie was still very cold and rainy at the time, I'm sure Andrew and Fergie would have not care much about being wet but I did not want them to be sick so we played inside the very tiny apartment. Fergie was six at the time and Andrew was already eight years old but they were still full of stamina, poodles keep young for a long time.

July 20, 2006 Fergie in the new basement couch

• •

That same Year shortly after we moved to Canada, we were able to purchase a house, here is Fergie in her first picture sleeping in the brand new couch we purchase for the basement TV room. That couch is now long gone, yes my dogs ruined it and we ended up replacing it, we always said the house belongs to the dogs and we are just their slaves, LOL.

As you can imagine my dogs are allowed on any single piece of furniture we own, if they want to jump on it and snooze they are welcome, this has always been my rule for my dogs so that's why when Fergie was showing everyone at the show's said she was spoiled, and maybe she is spoiled rotten but she deserves it, she is really kind and a good girl.

Andrew in our bed fall of 2006

Andrew our boy is now 15 years old and blind so he doesn't look like this anymore. He doesn't sleep in our bed because he doesn't like to share his bed with anyone. He doesn't like when a human moves in bed while he's sleeping, this makes him very angry and snappy so for that reason he has always have his own bed in our bedroom. Or should I say a couple beds, because he likes to go from bed to bed at night time. Andrew is a little bit smaller than my Fergie but still considered a miniature poodle.

Winter 2006 Fergie and mom
• •

This is us enjoying a cold Sunday in the house, watching movies in the TV room, as you can see Fergie was comfortably lying next to me, and Andrew was not far on the couch. We spent many winters inside until we finally got used the snow and snow did not stop our day to day activities, especially because in Canada six months of the year are snow and cold, so we "adapted".

Ricardo and Fergie winter 2006

This is Ricardo having a moment with Fergie, yes Fergie was my dog until I married Ricardo, or pretty much until I started dating him, and she loves her daddy more than anyone in the world. Here is a funny story, back in 2004-2005 when Ricardo and I were dating, one night Ricardo came to visit me at my parents' house, and mom and I knew Fergie was always very excited to see him but at night time she would always go to bed with whoever went to bed first. That night because she was showing us how much in love she was with Ricardo, we decided to put her to the test. Mom went to her room, I went to my room and Ricardo left. Mom and I were expecting Fergie to go to bed with either one of us, to our surprise, she followed Ricardo to the door, when he closed the door and left her behind she jumped on my mother's couches so she could reach the window and follow Ricardo, Fergie was walking on the couch looking thru the window, crying because on the other side was Ricardo walking to his car and leaving her behind. That minute I knew I had lost her, she made it clear she loved Ricardo way more than any of us, even though we had been her family from when she was 3 months old up until that day. I love Fergie very much and I pretty much let her choose me a husband, always trust your dog, if your dog doesn't like your boyfriend maybe you should not like it either. Dogs always go for kind people and that's who Ricardo is a very kind and nice guy.

To this day I have a deep connection with Fergie. Fergie taught me a lot, made me enjoy what it is to have a show dog that loves to show. She is a kind soul and a kindred spirit, she took Peachy under her wing, made me believe in female dogs again but I know her connection with her daddy is way deeper and if she has to choose she will choose him over me anytime. So I'm just smart enough not to put her on that position LOL.

Fergie and Andrew in bed

That's is us sharing a bed moment still during the winter of 2006-2007 that was our first winter so getting two feet of snow was not exactly nice for us beach people. LOL

Andrew waiting for his ball
• •

Andrew and Fergie at their best, Andrew waiting for daddy to kick the ball back at him, and Fergie just resting on top of her dad, in this picture Ricardo had probably kick the ball at least a 100 times for Andrew and Andrew was still wanting to play more. Andrew was a toy nutsy when he was able to see. Today he still plays but way less than before. We even have a video of Andrew playing soccer as a goalie with Ricardo, of course Andrew was a super good goalie, and no ball would ever pass him.

How I met Peachy
● ●

Summer 2007 and my twenty-eight birthday, I convinced Ricardo that all I wanted for my birthday was to adopt a little recue poodle, so looking on pet finder, this is the first picture I saw of Peachy and that was it. I saw and selected a couple more dogs from the website but deep in my heart I knew this little girl was coming home. There was something about her eyes that just said to me "I'm your new baby", and sure enough I started the adoption process.

The adoption process

I went on the website of the rescue that had peachy and this was her second profile picture with this description:

"PEACHY (F, 6 y/o), so named for her apricot color, is a tiny Toy Poodle. From a commercial breeding facility, she can be skittish at first; however, after being held for a while, she begins to relax. She requires a very quiet home where someone can work with her to further her socialization. She has the potential to be an awesome dog."

I still remember Ricardo was still reluctant, and he never thought I was going to get Peachy, we did the paperwork, the phone interview, the trip to pick her up and by August 5, 2007 she was home forever and our lives had been forever changed. The whole process took us about 6 weeks and thru the whole process Ricardo kept telling me, "just buy a dog, I don't get why you are going thru so much work to get that dog". Inside me I knew she was meant to be with us and as a seasoned rescuer, I liked that the adoption process was long because that meant the rescue was doing a great job at placing the dogs and not only giving them to the first person that showed up.

I often visit the website and look at her profile pictures, after having had the privilege of having her in my life for seven years. In this picture she is telling people, "this is home for me, I'm safe here and I'll die here". No wonder she was passed by so many adopters, and if you did not get it from the picture she will make it clear the minute you came to meet her, her body language was telling us "I'm not interested in you, go away, this is too scary"; but that only made my desire to have her as my baby stronger. Ricardo was still trying to persuade me to get a different dog, but my heart, mind and soul was set on Peachy.

Peachy on the way home

Riding in the car for the first time

This is the first time Peachy travel with us; this picture was taken August 5th, 2007 on our way back to Sault Ste. Marie from Harvard, Illinois where we adopted her.

Peachy's first stay at a hotel

This is her first official Picture with her new siblings Andrew in blue and Fergie. She was still unsure about us, and we couldn't blame her, after she learned on her early years that humans were not to be trust.

Peachy's first bed

On the way back from Harvard, Illinois we had to stop at a hotel because we were not planning on driving nine hours straight, with our three dogs. Well it was Peachy's first night at a hotel and we didn't want her to be on a crate, but because that was all she knew, she chose the night table that resembled her crate.

I provided her with a pillow so she could sleep as a princess; after all I wanted her to realize that everything her life was, ended the minute I got her in my arms and from then on only the best we could provide would be given to her.

And of course she is wearing clothes. That little pink shirt was her first of many pieces of clothing she owned I found it at the local supermarket in Harvard Illinois, it has a crown on the back and read princess, I had to get it for Peachy this all happened the day we adopted her, from then on she was that "our little princess".

Peachy first trip

I wanted to share this picture because this is a good picture of her I believe; the picture was taken still on our way home, the day after we adopted her, she is sitting on the hotel bed not sure what is going on and for someone like me that has had rescue and rehomed many dogs in my life this was not normal, most dogs just move around and are happy to have a human in their lives but not my little girl. The look on her eyes tells me she wasn't sure, she just did not know what was going on, and after all she finally had made herself at home at the rescue. She had spent two years there and that was home for her, I can only imagine the many questions she had in her mind and yet she was fulfilling my lifelong dream of having a toy poodle. What better than a rescue one, little that I knew she was going to change our lives forever. From that day on, our lives pretty much revolved around her, finding ways to help her and keep her with us as long as we could.

Peachy's first home haircut

Well shortly after we got home, because it was the summer and it was "hot" I decided to give Peachy a haircut since she had been panting, well here she is in her first home made poodle haircut. She could not go to any of the grooming shops where we lived because they were just too busy and crazy, not even Andrew and Fergie went to get their cuts. Since we moved there I decided to start grooming my dogs on my own, after all I maintained their coats at home for the dog shows, so when we got little Peachy the natural thing to do was to give her haircuts at home. This, I agree, is not the best of many haircuts I gave her, she had only being with us for a couple days and looking back now I should probably just left her on her kennel cut. Oh well I'm sure she is laughing in Heaven right now about this terrible haircut.

Peachy's first blanket experience

I often put her on the couch with us; of course it started to cool down shortly after we adopted her and after I gave her that horrible summer cut, so I used to wrap her in a blanket so she would not get chilly while sharing a TV moment with us in the basement. Here she is sleeping wrapped in her blanket.

Peachy's first sweater

Peachy was wearing her first sweater here. I knitted her first sweater because she was so small that she needed something I could not find on the stores were I lived, not the best sweater I know. Later I learned how to make her a better one, but this one helped her thru her first fall and winter with us.

At that point she was not very doggie like, she was very quiet still, and she spent more of her days sleeping with Fergie.

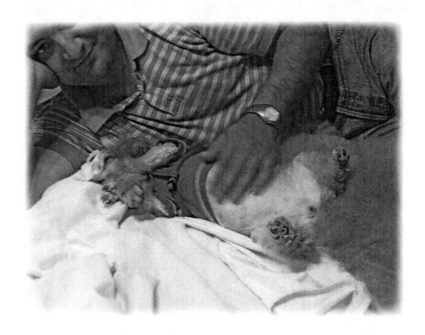

Peachy first belly rub

We of course put Peachy on our bed often, in fact the first night at our home, she was put in our bed to sleep, because that's where Fergie sleeps and Peachy only trusted Fergie, so the first night at home she was running around our bed and acting very stressed looking for Fergie, She probably also did not know what to do with her new found freedom.

So we decided to put her on our bed, it took her a while to settle but she finally fell asleep. This is back in September 2007 when she let Ricardo rub her belly for the first time; she was wearing an underdog T-shirt we got her.

Having her in bed was always stressful for us, because she did not had perception of altitude or how deep the fall would be, and we had to keep an eye on her overnight so she did not approach the corners of the bed and fell off it.

Peachy October 2007

Here she is in October wearing the sweater I made her and her collar with ID tag, well all I can say is giving her and ID tag was not a good idea, she still did not trust us and one time she ran into her crate to escape from me, because I was mostly at home with them and got caught in the wires with the ID tag. I of course panic and ran to help her immediately but if we would had not been home she could have had die that day. All because of the ID tag and we would have been devastated. The first months she was always vigilant of us, she did not want us close, so we were always careful not to get close to her while she was close to the stairs because we knew she would just fall down the stairs in trying to escape. She was so stressed out about being close to two strangers that she would rather throw herself down the stairs than being close to us.

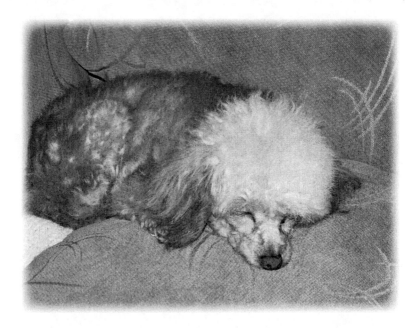

November 2007

Here she is, her fur finally grew back and she is sleeping in the basement couch, she used to close her eyes really strong at the beginning, she did not look very relax while sleeping, of course this was only her first months as a family dog and now I believe her panting was not because she was hot, but because of all the stress of living in a new home.

Peachy being more herself
• •

Here she is in September 2008 she finally started to be more of a princess and be more relaxed. She started to look for the softer and higher places to sleep while in the couch. She was a little angel.

Her first public appearance

I was at the time a huge fan of the local Humane Society and volunteered for them as well as fundraised for them. Here we are at the annual dog walk for the Sault Ste. Marie Humane Society. This was Peachy's first public appearance, about six weeks after we adopted her, I dressed her up as thinker bell and we took her for the 2Km dog walk fundraiser. She came with us every year and she always called people's attention because of her size, and because how unsure she was about people, this gave us the opportunity to tell people she had been a puppy mill mama and that she was still in her rehabilitation process. I see her as an ambassador for all puppy mill dogs, wherever she went, she ended up raising awareness with her story, people knew she was not "normal" and always asked us what was wrong with her, to us she was normal but I guess she was never normal to the eyes of the world. She was unique, definitely not a dog for anyone, she needed a special family, and we did our best to be that for her.

October 5th, 2008

• •

This is the first time Peachy ever took something from our hands, she was never interested on eating anything we offered her unless it was in her dish, but here she finally accepted to eat yogurt out of my hands, well sort off, as you can see I'm holding the yogurt cup with my arm stretched out as much as I can, and she is still keeping her distance. Peachy was very into food, and very into trying new things, she really enjoyed eating but as you can see here her fear for humans was stronger. Even though she had been with us for over a year she was still not sure about eating from our hands. Her biggest lesson to me "Be patient to who you love". And I'm still learning little Peachy.

Peachy's profile

I love this picture of her, this was taken fourteen months after we got her, but you can notice her lower jaw is slightly smaller, well she didn't had any bottom teeth left. When we got her she only had the two canines left in the bottom jaw, but her teeth were so decayed that were causing her a chin infection with a nasty open sore so the vet said the best was to pull out those bottom canines, he initially wanted to pull all her five teeth out, but I convinced him to clean the top ones and just take the ones that were making her uncomfortable, yes her three remaining teeth on the top were horrible too, but they were not causing her any problems yet and she seemed to use them. Sure enough, after her surgery to pull out her bottom teeth I remember the Vet technician telling me that when Peachy woke up in the recovery room, she was pushing her tongue kind of looking for her bottom teeth.

Gabriela Duran

Many puppy mill dogs are toothless as a result of not having any dental care or veterinary care, my little girl managed to keep her three teeth up until a couple months before her passing, she only had the two top canines and a molar on the top left side but if she needed to chew on something she would use her tongue and her remaining molar to get the job done. She made lemonade out of the lemons life gave her for sure. She was an example and a warrior.

Becoming a Therapy Dog

Peachy on her Therapy dog uniform

At the time we adopted Peachy, Fergie had been retired from the show world and had been certified as a therapy dog with myself as her handler, we used to visit the retirement homes and when Peachy came to live with us she used to see us go out every week for the visits and sometimes to events on the weekends to promote the Therapy dog program, Peachy had her animal communication session in the summer of 2008 due to her inexplicable seizures and that same fall I took some training in animal communication, at the training we contacted Peachy and she said it was her desire to become a Therapy dog.

Gabriela Duran

at her first Therapy dog public appearance

She said "Fergie told me and showed me what she does" and Peachy was exited to go visit the retirement homes and bring joy to old people. I remember the communicator asking her if she was sure because the testing to become a Therapy dog was really hard and Peachy replied "yes this is our job". Well I was really not sure how this was going to work because the Therapy dog testing is intense and dogs need to be walking on a leash and not been scared of loud noises and people, so even though I had thought about getting her certified I did not want her to be stressed out, but when she said that was what she wanted to do, we decided to give it a try and go for it.

The day of testing I was really stressed, Ricardo ended up testing with her and becoming her handler, she passed with flying colors. She was determined that she wanted to become a therapy dog and she survived the testing. This picture is at her first public appearance as a therapy dog the winter of 2008 and if you see her face she looks really happy to have the opportunity to give back. She was a big angel and a kind soul for sure.

Peachy summer 2009
● ●

The reason I want to include this picture of Peachy is to show you that even though she was a more much happier girl and she had been seen by an animal communicator a couple times, she was always with me, since I started working from home and she was also a Therapy dog as she wanted. She had seizures occasionally, we of course took her to the Veterinarian and he said her seizures were not long enough for her to be put on medication but she started getting her tongue hanging after all the seizures, is true she did not had teeth in her lower jaw, but we believe the seizures made her tongue hang a little more every year. She really only had like four seizures in 2008 and a couple in 2009, 2010, other than that she was a pretty healthy girl. I mean she had all kind of little accidents but that was because she was experiencing life, and when she finally was more confident she would jump off the couch like Fergie or try to go up the stairs on her own. She was a little bit of a dare devil too.

Summer 2009
• •

The summer of 2009, was the hottest summer we lived in Sault Ste. Marie, to the point that we ended up moving into the basement to sleep, we set up our inflatable bed in the TV room and of course Peachy and Fergie jumped with us on bed, in this picture Peachy was more trusting of me and she slept in my arms thru the night for the first time so that's why we took this picture and we believe is worth sharing it.

April 2010, Fergie's Birthday

• •

This is one of the many times we celebrated one of our dogs Birthdays, in this case was Fergie's 10th Birthday and Andrew and Peachy are by her side, back in 2007 we would have never been able to take a picture of Peachy like this one. You can tell by the picture Peachy is way more settled in to our family and way more trusting of us. That's how much she had grown.

December 2009

Peachy snoozing in the couch in the winter of 2009, she was getting way more settled, at this time she also started barking at us, she found her voice, when we first got her we were sure she has had been debarked, you know her vocal cords had being cut so she could not bark and bug anybody at the mill.

This did not surprise us because debarking is a common practice among breeders and puppy millers so we just accepted it, but one day she barked at us and from there on she had found her voice. She use her voice every time she wanted to eat or wanted something.

Her voice sound it like this "TAU, TAU" so we nick named her tau, tau.

She would normally get a little growl before barking and this would really make us laugh. It was like a little race car getting ready for a race.

Peachy and me

Here we are at the Annual Sault Ste Marie Humane Society dog walk in 2009; you can tell Peachy was more of a "normal" dog, she looks happy wearing her pink vest and her little crown. She always wore something different to the walk and well most times she ended up being carried thru the whole event, because her legs were not the best to walk a 2KM bush trail and she was also so tiny that for her own protection we would keep her in our arms so that way big dogs would not scare her. I love this picture because she is totally smiling in it.

My little puppy mill ambassador mama!.

Fergie and Peachy 2009

This is one of many pictures of Fergie and Peachy sharing a dog bed, like I said Peachy trusted Fergie from day one and Fergie took Peachy under her wing. Since the very beginning is like she knew Peachy needed a big sister, many times we would come home and find them sleeping together on the same bed. Peachy always followed Fergie, it was almost like Peachy looked up to Fergie to learn. They also did many things that they were not supposed to do, like getting into the laundry room find the treat container, remove the door from it (their treat container is a doggie food box) and steal from it. We called them Pinky and the Brain because poodle are smart by nature and Fergie was always looking for the opportunity to steal treats at our other house, so we called her the Brain and Peachy was always ready to second her in the stealing adventure. So many times we would come home to find them sleeping in a big doggie bed and treats scarce all over the floor with of course pieces of the treat bag around. Of course they had to wait until no one was watching so they had the time to do the whole thing, you know open the laundry room door, get to the container that was behind the open door, take the door of the container out and steal. So they made sure to at least eat some of the treats before being caught. Peachy was always innocent she only followed, Fergie was the master mind.

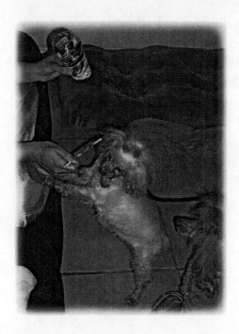

Peachy Begging for the first time on her hind legs.
• •

Peachy was continually learning how to be a dog, this picture is from summer 2010 the first time she stood up in her back legs to ask for food, she knew how to beg, well she learned from Fergie, and she improved the begging by barking so that way she was making sure you knew she was there and wanted to try whatever you were eating. But this day was the first time she stood on her hind legs to ask to try my frappe, of course I only let her try the wiped cream of it and she loved it.

At the retirement home with Daddy
....

Here she is in her happy face, at the retirement home, taking a break from visiting with her Daddy and her Sissy Fergie, of course they are both wearing barrettes, when Peachy came to us she had no hair on the top of her head and I could not put anything on it, but I let it grow and from there on, she always wore a pony tail with a barrette. Here she is also wearing one of her jackets. This picture is from the fall of 2009 and she has a happy face, so looking back at her pictures I believe we made her happy.

Peachy first Valentine's day
• •

This picture was taken February 14, 2008, her first valentine's day with us. I had gone grocery shopping and found this beautiful red polka dot dress with hearts on the belt. Of course I had to buy it for little Miss Peachy, she was still adapting to us. Adapting to get her picture taken every other minute and also adapting to be dressed up most of the time, but she did a great job looking at the camera. Don't you agree?.

Peachy's first Halloween picture
• •

Here she is in her cute pumpkin suit, it was her second Halloween with us, October 31 2008 and we decided to give everyone a Halloween custom and take pictures. The year before she had dressed up as thinker bell and Fergie as a princess, Andrew as an air force commander same costumes they used at the dog walk. But this year, we had found these costumes, little Peachy was not happy to be a pumpkin but she look cute, and Andrew hatted his devil custom for sure, he was in such bad mood. Good memories!

Peachy's first Christmas

Well we were living in Sault Ste. Marie so no Pet Smart there. In order to get this picture taken we traveled 1.5 hours to get our picture taken with Santa. It is a special picture because it was Peachy's first Christmas with us. She did great on the car trip. But at pet smart she had an accident, it was crazy in there because many people were there with their dogs and kids to get the picture with Santa taken, we had put the dogs in the shopping cart and Ricardo was in charge of them while I went to get in line for the picture. Ricardo had put Peachy in the kids seat of the shopping cart to keep a close eye on her, Andrew and Fergie were in the basket, well miss Peachy that was still not sure of people, jumped off the cart and Ricardo could not catch her, she landed on her back like a turtle and could not get up. I did not see it because I was getting in line for the picture but just to see the look on Ricardo's face when he finally got to me. He had Peachy

Peachy "The Warrior Princess"

in his arms and told me what had happened. Of course we did not hesitate since she did not show any signs of pain ever; we rushed her in to the emergency hospital inside the pet smart. They took x-rays and told us she was fine, no broken bones, at this time Peachy was still living in silence, she had not yet found her voice and with the doctors approval we proceeded to get our pictures taken with Santa.

Christmas 2008

This Christmas was uneventful, we managed to get our picture taken with the local Santa at the local mall, so we did not travel and we did not have a jumping adventure that year, everything went smoothly.

A new bed

• •

Back in the fall of 2010, Peachy jumped off our bed one more time, she had not done that in many years, probably since she learned that being in bed with us and Fergie was safe and ok. At this point my house no longer had carpets, we had removed all the carpets in the house because Peachy was not house trained and she would go, wherever she needed to go. When she needed to go, so in order not to stress her out, trying to house train her, we removed all the carpets in the house, after all she had had a couple accidents in the carpets and let's face it the house was an 80's house so it needed to be brought up to date. Peachy just helped us hurry up with our renos, like I said first thing to go was the carpets. So when peachy decided to jump of the bed that fall of 2010 in the middle of the night, we of course woke up when we heard the noise to found her on the floor, we were scared, thinking OMG she may had broken something. She did not have any scratches of any kind but in order to protect her the next morning I went to the pet store and bought her the biggest, nicest bed I could find for her. This picture was taken that same night while she was sleeping on her new bed. She loved that bed.

Even though she was not house trained, she would still hold it for hours if we were traveling in the car or by airplane, she never messed up the car and she used to ride free in the back sit with my other dogs. I got a special cover made for the seat that simulates a basket so Peachy would not fall off the seat if we had to brake suddenly. The interesting part is she would let us know she needed out if she was in the car, she would start panting and fussing and that way we knew she needed us to stop for a bathroom break. In the house she never gave us any signs.

Also the summer of 2010 we had bought a new bedroom set, changed our queen size bed for a King size, the new bed frame and mattress have a gap in between the headboard and the mattress, one of the first nights of Peachy sleeping with us in the new bed, she managed to get half her little body in the gap and she was going down through the hole, we of course were sleeping, but she started winning to wake us up, when we woke up and saw her half body on the hole and only her chest, front legs and head in the mattress, we rapidly pull her up and out of the hole but we were surprised she decided to make noise and wake us up. You see if this would have happened to her at the very beginning of her time living with us, she would had just let herself go through the hole and we would have found her the next day underneath the bed. She really learned and grew up over the years, after that of course we used pillows and put our arm around her every night so she did not get stuck into the hole again.

In the TV room September 2011

Here she is on our TV room couch, this couch was cover by a blanket, because even though when we changed the furniture I got, pet friendly furniture, it never occurred to me that in two years my dogs would peel off the surface of the couch LOL. Really rather than bugging us, we think this is part of being a pet owner, Peachy, Fergie and Andrew spent uncountable hours on top of that couch so really is now the doggies couch instead of the TV room couch, we do sit in it when we want to watch TV but usually we would have to find a spot where we did not bug the dogs.

This is also the couch Peachy jumped of in the summer of 2012 and broke her right top canine, Peachy knew how to get off the couch, learned to jump of furniture, even though we were always keeping an eye on her to help her down so she did not jump off, this day we were sitting next to her watching TV and she just jumped off, she landed badly, instead of landing on her legs standing as she always did, she landed face first and tumble down and then stud up, of course I was hysterical, ran next to her to see if she was ok, Ricardo is always more calm, we didn't see anything wrong with her but the next day I ended up taking her to the hospital because she had a little bump on her face, and when I tried to look at it she kept moving her face away, I saw her tooth was loosen so I rushed her to the Vet, sure enough the vet said she had broken her canine. The vet pulled the canine since it was just dangling from a piece and he did not want to put her under for that, but now after all that she went thru with that canine root that was left there I think it would have been better to put her under and get all her remaining teeth pulled out, perhaps she would have not gone thru the nasal discharge and she may be still with us, but we will never know.

April 29, 2012

Peachy sure loved her brown bed; here she is having a lazy day. She was always a go, go, go girl, but this day it was super cute to us that she did not feel like leaving her bed, she was not sick or anything. We had just come back from a trip and she had stayed at the pet resort with Fergie and Andrew so I guess this was her way of saying "Thank God I am home". This was the last time she stayed at the pet hotel after this trip we hired a nanny to come stay with them in the house whenever we travelled or we would take them with us as much as we could.

October 28, 2012
• •

Here she is coming out of her carrier, she had just recently recover from pneumonia and before the pneumonia, and she had recovered form a bite on her head. To this day we don't know what happened, as I said I worked from home so I was always keeping an eye on them and one day in August I picked her up to brush her and I saw she had this red spot on her head. I stop brushing immediately and ran her to the Vet, well it turns out it was not only a little red spot, when the Vet took a look at it she had a huge open sore, the size of a nickel, Vet said it was a dog bite, and the only one that could have done something like that to her was Andrew. Of course Peachy was put on antibiotics to prevent her from infection and I had to keep the wound clean. While cleaning her every day, I realized she also had some marks underneath her eye, I still don't know when did that happen, and why Andrew decided to bite her but to this day I feel like a neglectful owner.

She said it was part of her experiences and I did the best to keep her safe, still I would have wanted to keep her in a bubble so she did not had any of her experiences/ accidents.

In this picture I had taken her with me to a seminar, and she had just woke up and decided to show her pretty self.

Toronto, November 15th, 2011

This was Peachy first and only trip to Toronto, we had gone with Ricardo, and we are outside Toronto's Paws way center. This doesn't mean Peachy did not travel; she at least traveled twice a year to Detroit with us, because her brother Andrew has glaucoma and was being seen by an eye specialist there. We used to make a trip out of this, we started going to Michigan Veterinary Specialist (MVS) in 2007 and because we lived in such a remote location in Ontario, we used to make it a weekend trip. Later became easier when my niece moved to Detroit in 2012 because now we no longer had to stay at a hotel with the dogs. But before that Peachy had to become a pro traveler, in the car and in the hotel, she stayed at Hiltons, Westin's, Marriott's and best westerns with us. And every time people saw her at hotels, she would put a smile on them, being so little and being kept in long coat with bows, made people look at her all the time, she was a heart opener and as she said a healer.

September 1st 2012, Birch run

Here we were once again going to Detroit to see the eye doctor, we had stopped at Birch run to sleep because we had left Ontario late the day before and from Birch run is pretty much 1.5 hours to Michigan Veterinary Specialist. This is the best western in where we stayed many times on our way to Detroit. That morning Peachy was impatient. She had slept with me; we got a double room so we each took a dog in our bed and Andrew on the floor since he doesn't like to share his bed time. This morning Peachy wanted out very early and she decided to walk over me, she was truly a happy girl. Ricardo took that picture of her, she was barking, well doing her TAU, TAU noise we called bark and wagging her tail and running around the bed, it was time to get up, get her out for a pee and feed her, that's all she wanted. After she ate she would settle again.

This was a week before she ended up being hospitalized with pneumonia.

My trooper girl, she truly was an example, no matter what, she was happy to be alive and happy to wake up every morning, so she always celebrated, running around, barking or what I called "tauting", growling and jumping at our feet so we hurry with her meal and then waiting to be pick up and taken down stairs to eat.

Peachy at the Back yard door
. . . .

We took this picture back in 2011, after I had groomed her, Peachy was Peachy so, she did not like going outside, she was very uncomfortable in the back yard, that's why most of her pictures are taken inside the house. She did not like going for walks or being without a roof, so since we had few pictures of her outdoors and that day she was looking particularly cute. I took this pic while Ricardo held her up. She once said she felt unprotected outside and felt like an animal would come and get her, we really respected her a lot so we did not force her, all we did was our best to make her happy.

Peachy in Ricardo's arms

This is September 2012, not the best time for us, Peachy is sleeping in Ricardo's arms, I had been working home all day and noticed something wrong with her. She was quiet, not her usual self because she had develop this bossiness and every day around 3pm for the past couple years she would come looking for me to my grooming room, walk by the door a couple times, if I talked to her, she would go back to the TV room and wait for a minute to see if I was coming to serve her dinner. But if I did not talk to her, she would come inside the grooming room and start running around my grooming table, wagging her tail and barking at me, I would say "Peachy is not time yet, you have to wait till 5pm", she would go in and out of the room, barking wagging her tail, and running until I gave up and fed her dinner at whatever time she felt like having it, but on that particular day she had been quiet. Ricardo came home and I told him to keep an eye on her, she had dinner but she looks funny she doesn't want to lay down as usual, she keeps trying to put her head up, I left for a couple hours knowing Ricardo was home to keep an eye on her, when I came back I found her sleeping in his arms and that was it. I made Ricardo drive us to Emergency. Sure enough she had pneumonia, how did she get it, we don't know, but she never give us a sign, turns out her pneumonia was very advance and the vet did not gave us good outcome or any hope, she ended up being hooked to an IV machine and left in the hospital. That September 15th weekend was one of the worse we had lived through, we thought we were going to lose her for sure, thankfully she pulled through it.

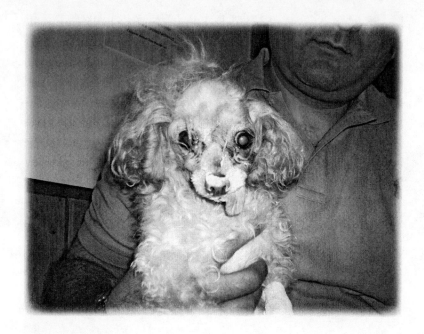

Yogurt face

• •

We took this picture at the hospital while she was recovering from pneumonia. The day after we hospitalized her, I went to see her and she did not look good, but she pulled thru it, because this picture was taken over the weekend on her second day at the hospital and she was already walking and eating, well she loved to eat. So we brought her a cup of greek yogurt and she just ate it all, she spent a couple more days at the hospital and after that she was discharged, with meds of course, but she survived pneumonia, until this day I think she was processing old emotions and this was just another layer of it. Someone else would had put her down maybe, but that is just not our style we fought for our dogs as long as they want to fight and stay here.

    I did support Peachy with energy work while visiting her, so that probably helped her too.

April 2012

Here she is in my old house kitchen, she was in the kitchen as much as she could, she knew her food came out of the fridge and she knew her meal times. Morning 6am she would be up, get out of the bedroom, go out to pee come back in and hang in the kitchen while Ricardo prepared her dish, then she knew she was going to be picked up by him and carried down stairs to eat. She knew her meal was serve in her crate that was the only time she was in a crate, so as soon as Ricardo put her on the floor she would run to her crate, jump inside it and bark while jumping until she got her dish. She would eat it all and bark again so we knew she was done eating and she needed someone to open the door for her so she could get out of her crate and run around looking for a bed to crash after breakfast. That was pretty much her morning. From her bed she would see dogs come in and out of the house to be groomed and she was just fine with it, she would come say hello if she felt like it. Or if not she would just hang with Fergie until it was her time for dinner, then she would look for me.

Peachy's last picture with Santa

Certainty when we got this picture taken to help the Chippewa county animal shelter, I never thought it was going to be the last picture with Santa or the last Christmas we would had Peachy with us. This is a great Picture, she looks so cute in her Christmas dress and she was very much into getting her picture done, it really took no time. We walked in at the local store where they were holding the fundraising, the girls were dressed up and ready, as soon as they got into Santa's lap they look at the camera. Peachy was a pro now, from the day we adopted her until the day she left us we took many pictures of her, and she learned the word "mira"(Spanish for look), so every time we wanted her to look at us we would say "mira" and she would just stare at us. Weeks after this picture, Peachy was enjoying Christmas at my parents' house in Mexico with us and her sister Fergie.

Peachy you were truly a cutie!

Peachy in Veracruz
• •

So last Christmas after not being home for christmas in six years we decided we would spend christmas in Mexico. We took Peachy and Fergie with us. Andrew had to stay due to a minor surgery he had to undergo. He stayed recovering at the hospital. Unfurtunatly I don't have pictures off the whole ordeal, since we ended up living home on december 22 driving to Detroit were we stayed at a friends house with our dogs and then from there catching an airplane to Veracruz. We had one stop in houston Texas, this was Peachy's first airplaine ride ever, and she did great!. I don't know for sure if she was excited, but she behaved like a pro. Fergie well this was one more of her many airplaine rides after all she came to Canada from Mexico an had traveled back and fort many times. But our little Peachy behaved amaizinly. We were worried she was going to bark as soon as she smelled food on the airplane and she did not. We fed her at Houston airport, there is a mexican restaurant on terminal E where Ricardo and I had dinner while waiting for our airplane and we order the girls grilled chicken, so they could have dinner to. LOL. She had grilled chicken and rice and as always she cleaned up her dish.

I love travelling thru the USA because they are more used to having people in airports with their dogs and that certanly made it easier. Rather than looking at you as the weirdo, who is traveling with their dogs, they see you as a person who is traveling with their family. Often flight attentdants comment on how well behaved my dogs are, because of course they travel inside the cabin so we can keep an eye on them at all times.

As soon as we landed in Veracruz, we were picked up by my family, my cousin found it interesting that the dogs were wearing diapers, well that way if they needed to go, they could go without any trouble. It's a long ride from Canada to Mexico specially because we go all the way to Veracruz so I couldn't ask my girls to hold it. They know they can go on their diaper, we took them for pee brakes when we are at airports in between flights. But still they have the diaper as an option.

I was trully worried for Peachy, since it was a new adventure, she had travelled with us a lot, but always in the car, so going on an airplane was totally new and being confined in her carrier all day, that was the part that worried me the most. But it was like she knew, I'm sure Fergie told her what was all about because Peachy just slept in her carrier all the way, and when we landed in Veracruz at 11pm that night she had no interest on getting off her carrier, she rode in the car all the way to my parents house sleeping in her carrier and as soon as we arrived home she started investigating the place with Fergie.

Fergie knows my parents house very well since she lived there for six years before we moved to Canada, so I'm sure she taught Peachy everything about the house, the dogs that live there and the people, because Peachy behave like she knew the place.

December 23, 2012

This picture was taken at my parents house in my bedroom, I guess the trip to Mexico had been a little hard on little Peachy's body because here she is the morning after in our bed, slepping and not really wanting to get out of bed. I do often tell Ricardo now that she is no longer with us. Do you think we were good parents, I mean she had many accidents thru the years with us? And Ricardo often tells me, "yes because she finally lived, she went everywhere and you took her up and down all the time so of course she would had accidents, she was finally not confined to a crate and was living".

And I even asked Peachy when she visited me the morning after her passing if we had been good to her, I also said I'm sorry you had so many accidents, she replied "Mom, those were part of my experiences, I didn't know many things when I came to you and I learned over the years, the accidents where part of it, but you did the best you could" she also said to Kumari when Kumari asked her if she had a good life Peachy replyed "yes, it was a pretty good life and now I'm ready".

Peachy truly had all kind of silly little accidents like bumping on glass doors at MVS because she did not know they were there, banging her right eye last time she stayed at the pet resort, and of course as the over protective mom I am, I decided she was no longer going to this place. Jumping of furniture, chocking on her own food because she was rushing to clean her plate, fell backwards, and most recently because her legs were giving her problems fall on her back often. But when she fell on her back this year at least she decided to use her voice and she would scream to call us so we hurry to her side to help her get up. She was rarely alone, there was always one of us with her in the house or in the hotel since we lived there for six months.

At grandma's snoozing with my Sissy
• •

Here they are sleeping together in my bedroom; this was the remaining of what once was Fergie's bed. The original pillow had been thrown away by my mother but she still had the plastic basket and gave the girls and old pillow. Really she gave Peachy and old pillow for that bed because mom knows Fergie has always slept with us on our bed, and well Peachy ended up sleeping in bed with us too. Because we were using the AC and Peachy was ok with us in bed, she actually like it, but when we were out and about and no one was home, the Girls were put in my bedroom with the Air Conditioner going, and Fergie and Peachy would get themselves together in the little doggie bed and snooze until we got home.

Peachy was truly a heart opener, because she would open the heart of people that don't like dogs like my mother, my mother who is not a dog lover was totally in love with Peachy. Everyone that met

Peachy was the same, while in Veracruz for three weeks the nurses that take care of my dad at night time, fell in love with Peachy. They call her "la viejita" (Spanish for little old lady), because Peachy would be running around the house, lay down somewhere in the living room and her little head would start to fall down as she fell sleep, Peachy of course fought it because she knew she was around people, so to the nurses, Peachy reminded them of a little old lady.

At grandma's Begging

Here we are, early morning and Peachy saw me eating a piece of bread, well she had already had breakfast but she never lost an opportunity to eat. She decided she was going to ask me for a piece. Yes I know a lot of people find dogs begging not a good habit but the truth is I was born and raised in Mexico with a father that is a dog lover and feels dogs should eat better than kibble, and should try everything their humans eat, so, I have always let my dogs try what I eat. If they are interested on trying why not?. So far I have not yet had a dog that dies of food poisoning or eat something they should not eat and get sick. In fact my dogs eat raw food now and the benefits I see on them are amazing, plus of course whatever they beg for.

At my parents' house the dogs have a basic kibble diet but they also eat table scraps, plus every time my dad eats something he shares with the dogs. The result, the dogs are pretty healthy seniors, so based on this I do let my dogs beg. Andrew and Fergie will come at the table and sit next to whoever is eating until the person gets tired of them staring and gives them something.

Peachy, well when she arrived to us, there was no way she was going to get close to us no matter what we were eating or doing but, over the years, she started taking treats from the fellows at the retirement homes while she was working as a Therapy dog and later she found her voice and learned by watching Andrew and Fergie that if she came close to us while we were at the table, she would get something of what we were eating.

When she started barking, she came and used her voice so you knew she was waiting with Andrew and Fergie next to your chair to get something from your plate, she was not patient when it came to food, she was very determined and if she wanted something, she wanted it now.

The begging with Peachy escalated over the years, to the point that she would run to the table as soon as she saw food coming at the table, stand next to the chair and jump, while barking and growling at us. She would also do laps around the table. Well to us was funny and also cute because she finally was showing some emotion, nothing made her more happy than food, food of any kind, food being served to humans, food being served in her dish, and because we encouraged her rather than force her out of the behavior she became bossy to the point that no one in the house could eat anything without Peachy being aware of it. She would run toward us to have a piece, she tried it all from fruit and vegetables to meats, tortillas and cakes, you name it she had it.

She also learned to use her ears, if she heard a noise in the kitchen or a wrapping been open, she would get of her bed and run to the stairs to bark, this was if she was downstairs, she knew that someone would come to pick her up or at least bring something of what we were eating down for her to try.

At my parents' house she quickly learned her way to the kitchen. She also learned to stay close to my dad at the dining table, and as soon as she saw no one was at the table, she would go to the kitchen too ask my parents cleaning lady for whatever she was eating. Fortunately my parent's cleaning lady and nurses are all dog lovers and they were so happy to see this little tiny fur ball with all her physical limitations ask them for food.

The latest thing she did was, stepping on our feet barking, jumping and growling at us, while we were trying to prepare her meals so we hurry up, and also what we called the shark dance, at dinner time she would go in circles around our feet so we would hurry with her dish.

We miss her so much because she was the noisy and bossy little girl.

Peachy had one big passion in life and that was food. We really encouraged that passion and all the mist behaviors because, how can you really deny food to a dog that had a rough start in life?, how can you tell her she can't have what you are eating, when you know she probably starved many times at the puppy mill.

We celebrated with her and laughed with her, also encourage all her food begging. To us it was amazing that she kept finding ways to show her excitement for food.

In fact one of the things she said in her last communication while she was very sick was "stop all medical care, but don't stop the food!", "keep the food coming". And that's what we did, she even had breakfast the day she left us, so she went with a full belly.

At grandmas trying my new snow suit

Well my mom is a pretty good seamstress and I asked her to make Fergie and Peachy a snow suit. Thinking on our move from Ontario to Alberta and also influenced by the Ontarians that told me Alberta winters were brutal. So since we were in Mexico, and the girls were there, why not get them a custom made snow suit made by grandma. My mom surprinsily agreed and this is the result.

Unfurtunatly Peachy did not live enough to use her snow suit. We moved to Calgary in february 2013 and it was cold but not so bad that they needed the suit. Specially because we were living in a hotel suite. So really the grounds were kept spotless, as soon as the snow fell, there was someone cleaning it. so this is the only time Peachy wore her granys snow suit.

Coming back from Mexico, In Houston airport tram January 2013

• •

In the red plad carrier is my little Peachy behaving like a pro, and in the beige/blue bigger carrier is Fergie who makes herself small in order to fit under the airplane sit and not travel in cargo. Both of them happy after spending a month in sunny Mexico but sadly we needed to come back to Ontario, to pack the house and move.

Sleeping at Mariana's January 2013

Well we landed in Detroit, we picked up our car at our friends house and went on to visit my niece Mariana. She's been living in Detroit for the past year. Our vacation did not end just coming back from Mexico, we ended up spending two nights at Mariana's and Peachy decided that she was going to try the puff seats, you know those big round balls call puff. My niece has two of them, Peachy and Fergie loved them. We thought she looks super cute sleeping in the puff so here she is.

At my old house January 2013

We finally made it to our old home in Ontario; here she is sharing a bed with Andrew. I got that bed as a gift at a grooming gala and Peachy loved it. She used to get all the way up and sleep right in the middle of this bed. My little angel girl. She had about four different beds in the basement and a few different ones in our bedroom. This was the biggest bed and she always ran to it first, the rule among my dogs is whoever gets it first can have it and the others need to find another spot. Peachy usually shared with Fergie, but seeing her in the same bed with Andrew was uncommon.

At the residence inn

• •

Here she is at our first home in Calgary, a little hotel suite at the residence inn by Marriott, she is laying by the bedroom door. For some reason Peachy did not like to sleep in her beds anymore, maybe because the hotel was all carpeted and she could sleep in a soft place anywhere she wanted. She did have her routine and at the hotel probably because there was movement all the time she ended up waking up earlier than normal. Her usual wake up time was 6am eastern time, and since we moved to Alberta she started waking up at 5am. At the suite, she decided that she was not only not going to sleep in her bed or in bed with us but she was not going to sleep in the bedroom, she used to sleep in the living area looking at the bedroom and at 5am she would get up and start walking towards the bedroom to see if we were up to feed her. If we didn't move she would go back and snooze for a while and try later but if we moved, that was it, she would run around, bark, wagging her tail, doing her breakfast celebration so we took her out and feed her. My other dogs couldn't care less, if you sleep all day they would sleep all day with you, hold her pee and hunger and sleep, but not Peachy she had her times set, and breakfast and dinner time was what she lived for. LOL.

She also was very happy to be alive and free one more day, so that's why every morning was a celebration for her. That's one of her teachings "wake up every day happy to be alive, be grateful for your breakfast".

Cuddling with my dada

∙ ∙

This is one of the few pictures of her cuddling, taken February 2013, she did had a nasal discharge that took a while for the Vets to figure out what was wrong with her. Her nasal discharge started a couple weeks after we came back from Mexico, we took her to her Vet at the time and he put her on antibiotics because he thought she may be relapsing with the pneumonia, it did cleared out so we thought she may had had a cold. We moved to Calgary and a month after she started having the nasal discharge again, so we found her a really good Vet in Calgary.

The new veterinarian believed it was her teeth but since Peachy was old and her medical history was long, she decided to give her antibiotics and see if that helped her clear it out. In the meantime Peachy started being depressed and having small seizures while eating, we believe all that mucus did not let her breath well while eating and she was lacking air creating the seizure that went away as soon as she moved away from the dish and breath.

I contacted the animal communicator again because at some point Peachy was so depressed that she did not want to eat, so I thought it may be it, well turns out after her session with the communicator Peachy accepted to see a natural path for dogs for her nasal discharge and if that did not help her, then to get her remaining teeth pulled out, but her attitude was again happy girl, she started eating again, and walking and being happy.

May 15th 2013 my Birthday celebration at Residence Inn

This was Peachy's last Birthday cake, she turned 13 on May 15th, she had her teeth pulled out and was starting to have troubles with her left front leg, so we were taking her for laser acupuncture therapy to help her with her leg. Now looking at this picture she looks not so healthy anymore. From here, her health pretty much started to go downhill. She did get to eat a piece of her birthday Cake that day. I would have loved to be in the new house by then and have her celebrate her birthday here and have her enjoy the house a little more.

At the dog park June 2013

At the dog Park in June 2013, we stopped at the dog park while on our way to her laser acupuncture therapy, as you can probably tell her left front leg was not doing great here. She had no teeth left and well she was ok, but not thrilled to be in an open space, we pretty much took the picture and got out of there.

At laser acupuncture therapy for my legs

Here she is at her laser acupuncture session; she loved to go for acupuncture. After the session they used to wrap her in an infrared blanket and she always had this smile on her after the sessions. She used to fall asleep during the sessions and had a smile in her face.

I really believe she loved been treated, I often think of this as the equivalent of a massage for a human.

August 17th, 2013: first night at the new house

Peachy was already wearing diapers and not walking a lot, her back legs were not helping her, and her front left leg was not good either. We had stopped laser acupuncture at the end of July since we were not seeing her improve at all. She is seating in my kitchen counter while I take the pictures. We had just moved into the house and I still wonder if there was something else we could have done to help her. Her Veterinarian is sure she had something going on in her brain and that was why she started losing the use of her legs. This didn't help her because she started losing weight, having trouble going to the bathroom. I wish we would have been able to help her, and I wish she had recover her mobility and I wish we still have her here with us.

August 28th, 2013

Here is Peachy in her bed in my bedroom, Fergie jumped in bed with her. At this point Peachy was no longer mobile and we had to carry her everywhere, she pretty much had one good leg, her front right leg. I believe Fergie knew Peachy was going to leave her soon because Fergie tried to stay with Peachy as much as she could, jump in bed with her, be close to her, at all times.

Little Peachy I wish we knew you were leaving us shortly after this picture, we even started to fill our bath tub and get with her in it so she could move her legs but, rather than helping her, Peachy used to get really stressed, she was never in love with water, and I knew something had happened at the puppy mill that made her hate water.

After her passing she came to me and told me why she hated water, she said while living at the puppy mill, someone tried to drown her and because she fought for her life and survived, this person ended up giving her to the rescue. This did not surprise me since drowning dogs to get rid of them is a common practice among puppy millers.

Feeding time! September 2013

This is how we used to feed Peachy. Since we moved in to the house, she was no longer able to stand and eat from her dish hanging outside her crate, she was still in good spirits, eating good and wagging her tail, so we were feeding her in the kitchen counter. We used to hold her and hold her dish so she could eat. She was a trooper and will not get her face out of the dish until she cleaned the dish up.

September 24th, 2013

Here we are with her at the Veterinarian to get her eye ulcer rechecked, she had an ulcer in her right eye a week earlier and the ulcer was pretty big. When we came home from work I found her laying on her right side and I knew something had happened. Sure enough I picked up and she had her right eye close, I knew she had injured it, so I called her Vet, We took her to the clinic and the diagnostic was a huge ulcer on the right eye. The Vet gave her medication to help her heal and ask us to come back in a week to see how was she doing, during that week she seemed to be improving, the only thing was she kept having episodes where she woke up in the middle of the night scared and tried to run away. She could no longer walk so usually Ricardo would wake up and stay with her until she calmed down and fell asleep, her episodes became more intense and we started to take turns in the middle off the night. We even realized that if we fed her, she would calm down and fall asleep. Friday prior to her eye recheck we had gone to emergency at 4am since Peachy had been screaming for over an hour and nothing we did calmed her down. As soon as we got to emergency and her veterinarian took her she calmed down. Needleless to say this Tuesday during the recheck the vet said Peachy's eye was not improving and to make matters worse she had an ulcer on her left eye too.

She recommended a minor procedure to help her heal but she also said Peachy was at risk of having the right eye rupture, and if that happened her options where surgery to remove the eye, which she did not recommend or euthanasia.

To me Euthanasia was not an option, is my last alternative, I first want to do everything possible and impossible to help my dogs.

Peachy had a session with the animal communicator the Monday before; because she had been having screaming episodes in the middle of the night for over two weeks and I was worried. I wanted to know if it was emotional and her communicator could do something to help her or if this was as the Veterinarians said the end.

Peachy said she was preparing to transcend and she did not want any medical care anymore. She wanted to be provided with a confined place. Turns out animals practice how is it to live in spirit, and go back and forth, in and out of the body and is easier for them to do this if they are in a confined space with a roof. No wonder Peachy had been behaving strangely and we had found her many times since we moved to the house underneath my bed or the treadmill or behind a couch. She said to her communicator she wanted something round I immediately knew what was she talking about, and that she was going to go on her own, but no more doctors. Peachy also said, "I'm not healing, because is no longer important to heal the body".

My human part took her for her eye recheck and I think that's why we lost her. So a hard learned lesson to me is "I should had listened to her, and not taken her for her eye recheck", maybe we would still have her with us today.

Gabriela Duran

    That day after the recheck we were given a referral to see the eye specialist in town. Probably a little too late for us.

    Next time when one of my dogs says no more doctors. I'll honor their request. Animals know when is their time to go, and unlike us humans, they are not afraid of the trip, not afraid of leaving their physical body. They know there is more than the physical.

The practice tent

This is what Peachy was referring to, when she told her communicator she wanted something soft and round to practice being out of the body. I immediately went to get this out of the basement so she could use it as much as she wanted. Sadly it was too late. She only lived 3 more days after her last animal communication session and I still believe we cut her life short by taking her to get her eye rechecked.

September 26th, 2013

At the emergency specialist center, we went in to see the ophthalmologist. Since we had been told by our Vet that any eye emergency coming in to the hospital was seen by the eye doctor. We walked into the hospital at 8am after not having slept at all, since Peachy had been screaming all night. We thought she was in pain.

They took forever to receive us and when they finally did, a regular emergency doctor came to see Peachy, turns out the ophthalmologist was not in until the evening since he teaches at the University. Well we thought ok, they are going to give her something for pain so she relaxes and sleeps while we wait for the eye doctor. Turns out we ended up staying with her all day at the hospital while the emergency doctors looked at her, went back and forth, ask if it was ok to do blood work and urine analysis because she may had something else wrong. They did all the studies only to find out her blood and urine where normal. While at the hospital the worse happened. Around noon time I saw blood on Peachy's eye and I knew her eye had rupture, sure enough, the emergency Vet just confirmed it. I honestly was not impressed by the service we received at the emergency specialist veterinary care facility because I felt they did not do much for Peachy. Nor they wanted to do anything for her, because she was old and had issues with her legs, the first thing the Emergency Vet said was "I think you should consider putting her down". In all this commotion I ended up getting a hold of Kumari, Peachy's animal communicator and healer, and I'm glad I did, because she was with us thru the whole process. She checked with Peachy and Peachy said it was not pain, but she could not see and that was really freaking her out. Kumari explained to Peachy that she needed to calm down and that we were waiting for the eye specialist. Peachy said "if I'm not going to be able to see, then I don't want to live". I even told Kumari to please explain to Peachy that many dogs live blind and are ok, Andrew for example has being blind for many years. During the day Kumari kept in contact with Peachy and with us, and by the time we saw the ophthalmologist at 530 pm he said, "the right eye is gone there is nothing to do but to remove it, and due to her age I don't think she will survive the procedure, the procedure is very painful and has a long recovery time, and we will probably have to do the same with the left eye after so my recommendation is to let her go".

For Ricardo and me it was like hearing the ophthalmologist said to us that we needed to kill our baby, so we talked to Kumari and she said well Peachy wants to go and she is ok with you guys helping her go. She said she is done, done with this body and ready to go. Really because Peachy had been screaming pretty much 24 hours nonstop we decided to honor her wishes and let her go, but we are still humans so, we didn't want her to go right there. We talked to the eye doctor to see if he could give her something to control the pain so we could take her home for the last time and arrange with her regular veterinarian for her euthanasia. The ophthalmologist gave us pain killers and we got in our car and rode back home. Probably the worst thing we could have ever done.

Peachy's last bed

Because Peachy could not stand to be on one of her beds anymore, and moving around in the carpet was really irritating her skin on her legs, we used to put her in a soft blanket. But because she used to go out of the blanket and into the carpet where she could injure her skin by rubbing it on the carpet, we came up with the idea to keep her in an enclosed area made with pillows so she could not get injured. In this picture Fergie is visiting Peachy, like I said she was looking for her all the time, that should have given me the clue that Peachy was leaving us, but my motherly love and my humanity kept me in denial.

September 27th, 2013

We took Peachy home on the 26th from the emergency hospital, with pain killers, this was a big mistake. Little that we knew the pain killers were not going to work, because as she told Kumari. She was not in pain she was freaked out that she could not see. Part of me told me to just euthanize her at the emergency hospital, because I could no longer hear her cry, my heart was shattered from all her crying, and me not being able to help her. But Ricardo felt it was not the right way to do it. He felt Peachy at least deserved to be home with her sister Fergie, and Fergie deserved time with Peachy, so I agree to take her home. By 11pm that night I was calling Peachy regular Veterinarian to let her know what was going on after all she had not been able to treat Peachy when we came in the day Peachy got the eye ulcer. Peachy had been treated at her normal clinic by the other Vet not her regular Vet, so when I called her at 11pm while she was working emergency, and I explained the whole situation. That the pain killers where not working, and that we had appointment to see her at 5pm on the 27th for euthanasia, she said "I believe, there is nothing to do, I knew she was going to go but never though it was going to be her eyes and if you want I can make arrangements so you can come in earlier"

I went back to talk to Ricardo about it and I said I was going to move the appointment for 9am. I took this decision with great remorse and grief I felt like I was playing God, but I knew we needed a miracle to save Peachy and I could not hear her cry anymore, I had vowed to protect her and I felt I was failing. We took turns and stayed up all night with her, she slept for about two hours that last night. Of course we were very emotional, I was crying like a mad woman, praying like crazy and deep inside I knew it was the end, I knew no matter what I did, she was leaving us.

Peachy at the hospital waiting for her catheter

Fergie stayed next to Peachy the whole night and the morning of the 27th, Peachy still had breakfast before going in.

At the time we were leaving for the hospital Fergie decided she was coming, and she sat in front of me and looked at me, I knew she was saying "I'm not staying behind in the house, I'm coming with Peachy"

I told Ricardo Fergie wants to come, and she is coming. We got in the car and drove to the hospital, I held Peachy all the time while Ricardo did all the paperwork. The Veterinarian that had been giving her laser therapy came to give us support, because I had called her at 6 am to let her know what was going on. She was kind enough to come, this helped, because at some point the vet technician came to take Peachy to put a catheter on, and her rehab Vet went with her to the back room. They came back and gave me Peachy back. It was like she knew, as soon as she came back she stop screaming.

Minutes later her Vet came in with the injection and explained us what was going to happen, she said "I will basically over dose her until her heart stops, you may see her body twitch afterwards, is normal as the muscles are relaxing". She asked me if I wanted to hold her and to my surprise I said yes.

That was the last thing I could do for my little girl, have the courage to hold her in my arms while she was leaving her body.

It just felt right that Peachy did not leave this world alone, she was surrounded by her rehab Vet, her dad, her sister Fergie and in my arms. She was at peace, but I was just crying I felt like I was losing a child. She went peacefully; she did not fight the chemicals.

I kept her in my arms and she looked like she was sleeping, Ricardo also held her for a while and after a while we deposited her in a doggie bed. They had prepared for her body and she was covered with a teddy bear blanket and taken away. We went home with Fergie and it was a terrible day for all of us.

Gabriela Duran

Peachy last Picture in her daddy's arms

That night I fell asleep and I dreamt with her, I'm grateful she came to visit me an answer many questions I had, and from there on we could feel her around in the house, especially in the kitchen.

Ricardo said that while preparing the dogs meals, he felt deep sadness and all of the sudden she was there with him making him smile. I have felt her going up and down the stairs in our house, and even saying "Mom look now I can walk again". Ricardo also once told me she was with him during a dog walk.

One of the things Peachy said about the day she left was "Mom the room was full of angels and I was on the angels arms watching the whole scene, I was no longer in my body, Fergie was holding the space for me, and of course they gave me wings" in an excited voice she said "I got my wings immediately mom, but I made the angels carry me to heaven, you know I have to practice with these things" she made me laugh.

I know she is fine and doing great in heaven and that she may have been called because heaven most have been in need of an Angel but we still miss her, and we wish deeply we could have her around the house, bossing us, and barking at us for food.

Peachy was truly a warrior, she had a very rough start in life and lived many years of abuse and neglect that ended up cutting her life short. But she found a way to overcome all the sadness and live life with passion and intensity. Taking every experience in full and learning, she was constantly learning, and she was constantly making lemonade out of the lemons life gave her. Peachy's life would have been very different if instead of having been born and slaved at the puppy mill for 5 years she would had been free earlier or would had been born free, but as she said "this was my life, my journey and I had a great life"

That says a lot of you little girl, having categorized your life as "a great life".

We love you Peachy and you know you are welcome in our lives anytime, so until we met again little one, until we met again.

Resting in Peace covered by a Teddy blanket at the hospital

After Peachy

On October 2nd, I got the call to pick up Peachy's ashes, her little box lays in our bedroom with her little ID tag on the top, but deep inside our hearts we know that was not the end, it was the beginning for her, and as difficult as it is for us as humans to not have her around in a physical body, that we can hug, we know she is still with us in spirit. Our greater teacher and as she once said our healer. I do believe little one that you are a healer and as you said "I'm quite advance as a healer".

I hope you love the story because is a story of love. I honestly after having Fergie never thought I was going to have such a deep connection with another dog, and all I can say is that my connection with Peachy was deeper. She was my teacher. I adopted her thinking I was rescuing her and in reality she rescued me, forcing me to open my world to the world of energy, to see beyond, be more open and be less afraid and judgmental.

Thank you little one.

Being comforted by my daddy, while at the emergency hospital

Peachy's leg

Remember that at the beginning of this book I said to you to keep your mind and heart open, and this is because what I'm going to write is not easy to digest if you don't have your mind and heart open. I'm not intending to make you believe but this has been my experiences after living with Peachy. Before Peachy I was pretty much a scientist, a snob and an elitist dog lover. Now I'm more open and I accept more things, I'm more open minded.

What made me open my mind? The answer is love, love for a little tiny fur ball that had suffered too much and needed help, and the only way I was able to help her was by getting involved in the world of spirit, by believing that we all have a soul. That not every illness is cured with conventional medicine. I had to see Peachy more as a soul that had suffered than an animal that had suffered and that was the only way I could help her.

To me was really hard to believe in animal communication, after all I am an Engineer with a Master in Sciences, so show me the scientific proof. I ended up going to the animal communication workshop in 2008 as a skeptic, there was proof already. Peachy had been treated by the animal communicator/healer and had changed, and improved.

There was some truth about this person been able to connect with my dog from another country and been able to know what my dog was going thru. What she needed. But still I travelled all the way to Mexico City and sat at the workshop.

My experiences, I was able to communicate with the animals in the group, and not only that, my dogs that were in Canada, showed up many times while I was practicing. At that point in my life I had so much anger stored for many things that had happened to me, and the anger was blinding me. But Peachy only seamed to respond to treatments with the animal communicator/healer, so because of love I just went with the flow.

Of course this also directed me to my own journey and to see inside what it was that I needed to heal. My progress has been way slower than Peachy's. Because my rational mind and my scientific training had put me behind many times. You know I was taking one step forward and then two back.

In 2010 I attended something called "I can do it" in Toronto and got myself a whole bunch of books, to my surprise the authors were doctors, psychologies, accountants, scientist, etc. that where all speaking about the same thing, having a soul in our bodies, everything is energy and being able to heal ourselves. Being able to get rid of the emotions that were causing us to be ill. Peachy was still being seen by a communicator/healer, she was not being seen all the time but when she had relapses of behaviors like the inexplicable seizures or look at us in fear, I knew it was time for her to get another fine tuning.

This 2010 conference even though opened my mind more and showed me that there were more people like me with some education that had just got in to the world of healing still made me reluctant. And yet, all my life I had been fascinated by the world of spirit. All my life I had gone to get readings, and believed in ghost histories but for some reason believing my emotions were making me sick was not computing in my brain.

Was not until 2011 that I finally enrolled in a program thru a Hay House Author and since then my life has improved so much. I have learned so much about energy medicine and how to heal with energy, that even though I still don't have the confidence to practice, it sure comes handy when I almost accidentally killed my dogs of heat stroke in the car back in the summer of 2011.

When that happened I had just come back from my very first workshop and I had just started meditating, so when Peachy fell on my arms the first thing I did was pray, "please God don't take her", of course gave her water and first aid, but after she came back I started using one of my energy healing techniques I had learned.

When Peachy had the pneumonia out of nowhere last year, again I used my healing techniques and pray for her, but I was sure this was just a huge layer of emotion she was processing. Of course we gave her medical aid and conventional medicine. In fact she was in the hospital for four days and every day I visited her, I did healing on her, so she felt supported.

Because I'm part of a group of healers in training now, I do asked for healing for Peachy every time something was going on with her and in this group many very talented and experienced people worked with her.

Most of my healing student buddy's that worked with Peachy said she has a beautiful soul, and beautiful energy and she would always be with me.

This year Peachy had a couple sessions with her communicator/healer Kumari to check and make sure Peachy was doing ok, and still wanted to be with us. We knew Peachy's body was old and all the neglect and abused she lived at the puppy mill had taken a toll on her but we also know now that life is about choices, so it was her choice to stay with us or to leave the physical plane and live with us in spirit. I cannot count how many times veterinarians asked me about my feelings on euthanasia, and told me I had to start thinking about putting Peachy down.

I can't tell you how I felt when at the emergency hospital the day before Peachy's transcending. The emergency Vet asked me if I had any religious believe that would conflict with euthanasia. I just kept my mouth shot, but truly I'm not God and as Maya Angelou Said "When I know better, I do better". So I knew if I had to euthanize my Peachy, it had to be her choice not mine.

Gabriela Duran

September 6, 2013: Daddy woke me up and was taking me down stairs for breakfast.

In fact the day we went to emergency at 4am in the morning her Vet said to us, "we needed to start thinking about putting her down", she said "Peachy may have a brain tumor and that's why she is having troubles with her legs". I totally respect our veterinarian and believe she is a really good doctor but she is still only human with a lot of scientific training so I can't judge her in fact I'm grateful to have her. Very few veterinarians have evolved into the world of holistic medicine and natural healing to name a few Dr. Martin Goldstein and his team who treated Peachy back in 2009 when she was having what it seemed to be "Cushing's". This totally gave Peachy a few more years with us. Conventional medication would have killed her. Or Dr. Melissa Shelton who I just met while having the honor to assist to one of her conferences. She is treating diseases with essential oils and saving lives with it, also training people and veterinarians all over the world.

You see before Peachy I did not have any of this information, nor I knew anything about energy medicine or was very spiritual, even though I had been raised catholic.

One of the things Peachy said on her last communication while she was still with us was, "it is not important to heal the body anymore", this only reassured me she had many times in the past healed herself and made the choice to stay with us. She also said "it's my time, I'm ready, I have completed my mission". At that moment I was filled with emotion and tears but now I think her mission was to awaken me to the world of spirit, to make me more human, to make me connect with my soul, and to make me publish this book to honor her memory and raise awareness, or as I like to see it continue with her mission of opening the hearts of people.

Its true I can still feel her around the house, and its true I'm still a little traumatized that it had to be her eye what took her, perhaps is because I have vision issues since childhood so I'm very sensitive to eye problems in my dogs.

I asked her the Saturday morning after her passing, I asked her about her leg, I said "why you were holding the leg back?". Because she started first holding the left leg back but after she also was holding the right leg back, my feeling was she was protecting her front legs. She showed me an image of her at a puppy mill auction where she was been shown to people, but the person that was holding her to show her, was holding her by the left leg almost as if he was holding a chicken by the legs.

She said "that's why I was protecting my legs mom, I was processing I needed to clear out things before leaving"

I really tried all to help her with the leg, or at least all that I knew according to the information I possessed then. Maybe, in a couple years I will have more information and I'll say "if I knew then what I know now..." but with the information I possessed, when Peachy was no longer responding to the laser acupuncture, I had her often in the energy medicine forum that I belong to so my peers will send her energy work. I went to Miraval the past July and I even consulted with a few healers there, did a group healing from Miraval for her, and every time, we were directed to pull from underneath her left arm, pretty ugly and disgusting energetic stuff would come out. But still that did not help her. I got a hold of a body talk practitioner for animals and she treated Peachy a couple weeks before Peachy's passing, her diagnose was, "Peachy is processing and as much as you want her to walk again she will not walk again. Give her some time, and stop the water therapy because that is only stressing her. It reminds her of old stuff and she could have a pneumonia relapse". So we stopped the therapy.

Peachy also said on her last communication, "I'm a healer, and I'm quite advanced, I'll be your guide and help you", perhaps that is why she was with me on my recent trip to Miraval, while I was getting some healing work done on myself, Peachy was right there with me, she was there during my meditations, she was there all the time.

To this day when I sit in meditation I can see her sitting on my lap with me, meditating. The same way we feel her around the house, we know she's still with us, but we still miss her physical body.

The morning she came to visit me she showed me she was doing great in heaven and she showed me many dogs I have had in the past. Many of my pets and many that I rescued and helped over the years. She even showed me her babies, the babies she was not able to keep alive at the puppy mill. She was truly happy in heaven and she had some messages from my other dogs.

As Penelope Smith said on her book "Animal talk", we all have the ability to communicate with other species; we are just so worry about what other people will think that we shot this ability down, because is not "normal".

My letters to Peachy

● ●

These are letters I wrote in my journal after Peachy left her physical body.

September 27th, 2013:

After a restless night Peachy, I decided to call the Vet to get you in for euthanasia early morning instead of waiting until the evening. You were in so much panic that my heart was truly torn with every scream you did. The pain killers they gave you yesterday were not good enough, they did nothing for you. You know my choice would have been to put you thru surgery and fix your eye, and then take you back to laser acupuncture to fix your leg but your plans were different. You did not want to be in this earth plane anymore, on Monday the 25th you told your communicator no more medical care, and yesterday when we took you to see the eye doctor. We did because you were in so much discomfort; you had not slept thru the night before. We did not sleep either, but that is not important, the important part was you, and we were so desperate that we did not know if you were in pain or having another episode of fear. Sure enough you told Kumari you were in fear because you could not see, and you did not want to live without sight. Peachy sight is not so big of a deal for doggies, remember Andrew your brother who is blind and he still moves around like nothing, but we love you and we respect your choice. I really believe we should have never let you had the kerotomy procedure I think rather than helping you heal, it made it worse, I believe that was what made you blind, and probably you would have been blind for the healing period but it was a really big deal for you my sweet angel. You decided not to fight back and to let the ulcer do a perforation on your eye and that was the end. I feel so guilty I feel I should have never taken you in for an eye recheck; I feel I should have let you, as you were and made sure you healed on your own. After all, you wanted to keep eating; you had such a passion for food. I was supporting your healing with energy work and prayers and you had healed and eye ulcer in the past. Little one, why did you go so soon, or why did we have to help you go so soon? You needed to be with me more, I love you and I feel lost without you. I feel you were still wanting to taste more stuff, eat different things, why couldn't you just go on your own, why the need of euthanasia? So many questions unanswered, so many blank pages and yet my heart is in deep pain.

This morning when we brought you to the clinic, you had been already overdose with pain killers and you were still screaming, you did have your breakfast because that was the only thing you never missed, meal time and appetite, no matter how sick or in pain you were. I would have liked you to be with us at least another five years, but heaven was in a big rush to get their angel back.

Sleeping in the couch at the residence inn, July 13, 2013

I was surprised that the minute they put the catheter in, you stopped screaming as if you knew what was coming, and then you just fell asleep, I find euthanasia horrible and maybe it was not your choice either but because of your eye and the trouble that was causing you, you decided that it was the way to go. So many things we did not do. I wanted to get you, to use your Canada pooch jacket and be happy at Halloween in your silly lady bug outfit and take you again for Christmas to Mexico but you decided to rest sooner than all the holidays. Doctors believe there was something going on in your brain and that was why your front legs were giving up on you, really the leg issue caused the ulcers, because you fell down could not get up and ended up scratching your eyes in the carpet. Having you in a crate all the time to prevent you from injuring yourself would have been horrible, especially because of all the years you lived in a crate at the mill, so we decided you had to be free always with us, I did take you to work with me but maybe not enough times. I so miss you very much and I so wish I would have been able to help you with the eyes and the legs issues. Why did you have to leave so soon? But you did leave in peace because your little tired old body did not fight it at all.

You were so full of light a true angel on earth that every single time people saw you, you inspired them to save a life, or put a smile on their faces with your little tongue sticking out. 13 years was a short life little one, your kind lives nineteen plus years but I do understand that all those years at the mill took a big toll on your body and shorten your life.

I'm so glad you chose me with your big eyes staring at me on that picture I saw on pet finder, the minute I saw you that July 2007 I knew you were supposed to live with us. And when we met you I can't forget you curling up like a little ball because you were so afraid of humans. But later you warmed up to us with the help of your sister Fergie who is missing you. And we were able to do the unthinkable with you, take you for trips, dress you up in little outfits, and make you feel happy, teach you to walk on a leash, teach you to ride on a car; you had your own stroller and many carriers. You even flew on an airplane all the way to Mexico and across Canada. You survived pneumonia and you kept going, you let me groom you and kept you in little fluffy cuts, have you wearing barrettes on your head. And you even smiled at your therapy sessions, you were a truly amazing doggie and I want you back so badly. I miss you little girl, even though it had only been 1 hour since your departure and even though I know you departed in peace. I miss your "tau, tau, tau" that you did to let me know I needed to stop everything and feed you, I miss you walking around the house, I miss you going out in the back yard and going up the stairs, something you learned but you never learned to go down so we were always careful you did not fall. I miss you a lot and I love you.

I miss when "tau, tau, tau" and running up and down the hallway in the old house was not enough you would be really annoyed and bark louder. I miss you coming to the stairs at 5pm waiting for your daddy to arrive and barking at him as soon as the door opened. I miss you been happy, been yourself. I miss how you discovered you could bark and started barking at us about a year into your adoption. I miss you biting my fingers when you took food from them, and looking at you closing your eyes while you closed your gums and bite me, you closed your eyes as if that would help you bite harder. I miss you being my little Peachy girl and I'm grateful I was able to be your mama.

You know I always wanted a toy poodle and I never thought I would get a rescue toy poodle that would teach me so much. Thank you Peachy girl for all the teachings and I hope you keep close to me as you did before, showing up during my healings and being love. I love you so much and in only six years you managed to be not only my special girl, also daddy's little girl, and you won grandma's heart too. Today you smelled like medications and that was never my intention, your top knot and ears were not fluffy because you did not like to be brushed anymore. Sorry if I kept you too long.

With all my love
Mom

April 18th, 2013. Here I am out in the patio of the residence inn

Ricardo's Facebook Memorial

Peachy
May 15, 2000 -September 27, 2013
Today an angel has gone back home.
Our little Peachy has left us to be in a better place.
God blessed us bringing her to our life and giving us the opportunity to give her love...

Visiting the dog park in Calgary, June 1st, 2013

"Rainbow Bridge"

There is a bridge connecting Heaven and Earth.
It is called the Rainbow Bridge because of all its beautiful colors.
Just this side of the Rainbow Bridge there is a land of meadows, hills and valleys with lush green grass.
When a beloved pet dies, the pet goes to this place.
There is always food and water and warm spring weather.
The old and frail animals are young again.
Those who were sick hurt or in pain are made whole again.
There is only one thing missing.
they are not with their special person who loved them so much on earth.
So each day they run and play until the day comes
when one suddenly stops playing and looks up!
The nose twitches! The ears are up!
The eyes are staring and this one runs from the group!
You have been seen and when you and your special friend meet,
you take him in your arms and hug him.
He licks and kisses your face again and again-
and you look once more into the eyes of your best friend and trusting pet.
Then you cross the Rainbow Bridge together never again to be apart.

Author: Unknown.

Gaby's Facebook Memorial

Tonight heaven will have a shining star, our little girl Peachy who we felt left us too soon. we know you were tired of living in an old body little girl an your passion for life made you fight the impossible, survive the worse and find happiness, we know your choice would had been to keep fighting to have more experiences but you decided yesterday that it was enough, you did not want to be blind and we had to honor your choice and let you go. I know you are still with us in spirit but the human part of me wants to hold you, and hear you run around and bark at me for your dinner. I love you sweet little angel and I'll always keep you in my heart. I'm grateful you choose me to be your mom and to give you silly dresses and trips and everything we could, I'm sure your sister Fergie is also missing you, but of course she knew it was your time, and she probably knew this months ago. In loving gratitude.

Mom.

Resting in one of my beds

October 5th 2013

Pepi, it has been a week since your departure and I still miss you deeply, yesterday was my mother birthday, I called her first thing in the morning, I know you said to write her a letter, I haven't done it yet. I'm still deep in sadness because I can no longer hold you in my arms. We just went to the movies and on the way there I pulled my cell phone and started looking at your last pictures, I know you were probably in pain because of your eye, I know you did not want your eye removed, I know you did not want to live blind but in those pictures you look so happy still in my arms, and after you passed away you look so peaceful and happy little angel. Seeing the pictures of you in my arms all happy while waiting for the vet to put you down, really made me think if we did the right thing, like I said I know your right eye was gone and needed to be taken out and I know you did not want that but still little one.

I know you came to me last Saturday and talked to me so I could find peace, knowing we did what you wanted, but still part of me wants to have you in my arms right now sweet heart, I feel like I did not hold you in my arms enough, I did not enjoy you enough, and even Ally your rescuer said that you would have not lived this long if someone else would have adopted you, your Vet said "we treated you as one of our kids and we went above and beyond for you little one", why would not do it for you, you deserved the best of the best, that's why we never regret any money we spent on you, my only regret is if I could have done more for you to have you at least a couple more years here with us. I know your body did not want to cooperate, and I also know you felt it was no longer important to heal the body. I know you were practicing being in spirit and see how it felt. I know it was your time but still I wish It would have not been your time and you would have healed the body again as you did many times before. I also know you don't want me to be sad, and you want me to celebrate your life, is just hard right now and I know you understand.

Gabriela Duran

Little one I never understood why your left leg went useless and even the therapy could not help you, I'm grateful that you showed me what happened to you on that leg at the puppy mill, and why you protected the leg so much and why later you also protected the other leg, of course conventional medicine did not have the answer, and probably doesn't have the answer for many puppy mill rescues, because having a puppy mill rescue goes beyond being able to provide veterinary care for it, and beyond being able to pay for the vet bills and all the things that can go wrong, not because you wanted, many things went wrong because you had no previous experiences and you finally experienced living free, walking around and being a princess dog, with that came some falls and minor injuries that required medical attention. I know it seems that we were always at the vet with you taking care of something but we did not care, we loved you and we wanted to keep you as healthy, happy and comfortable as we could, other injuries/illnesses were not so minor but were the product of the many years at the mill. Baby the minute I saw you on that website I knew you needed to live with us and finally experience living. The minute I met you at the rescue, I knew you were coming home with us, no matter what it took, and the minute I had you home and saw you having what vets call "seizures" in the middle of the night for no reason I knew veterinary medicine was not the answer and giving you drugs for seizures would have been totally wrong. Something told me that I needed to find a way to help you emotionally, I knew those seizures were flash backs from the years at the mill, so I'm glad I found an animal communicator and healer. I'm glad you opened my eyes to that world, because now when you come to me in my dreams or early morning, or when we feel your presence, I know is real, I know is you and I'm grateful for that.

Peachy "The Warrior Princess"

My last Morning at home, Mom is comforting me

I'm so very sorry for what you went thru at the mill, I would have given anything to meet you earlier, when you were a puppy and protect you from all that. But I also understand it was part of your soul contract, you needed to live in hell on earth first before being able to have it all and become our spoiled little princess, sweetheart. I always said you were a warrior, and it was hard for me to get why you were so terrified of water. Why you could not even get close to a water bowl and drink. Well when you showed me what they did to you at the mill it all made sense. I could not believe a "human" could try and drown a little angel like you, and clearly you fought for your life, your survived and were lucky that, that "human" didn't try to drown you again, perhaps one of your guardian angels make him/her stop and instead he/she surrender you to a rescue. Little one with us you were always safe, even though I know you felt the need to be vigilant when in the back yard or open spaces. I'll be waiting for you to come back to us as you promise, we all miss you, Fergie

Gabriela Duran

misses you the most, and daddy and me. Well little angel, what can I tell you, you took a part of our hearts with you and left us in deep sadness, we miss having you around in our bed, we miss feeding you, we miss carry you around, we miss being bossed by you.

Little wee one, I can't wait to see those beautiful eyes again.

Love mom.

Comfortably resting in my favorite bed, fall 2011

Peachy's Gift

September 29th 2013. An early morning with Pepi.

Well Pepi came to visit me again, of course we communicate with each other mainly early in the morning in my early awakening mode, I choose to still be in bed because I'm cozy there and she used to sleep in the same bed with us. Today conversation

I woke up and set my intention to communicate with Pepi my little angel and she came to me,

Me: good morning chiquiletin princesin (that was one of her many nicknames)

Pepi: very happy wagging her tail and smiling, "good morning mom, mom, can you see I have long hair again and they let me keep my crown barrette, I have all my teeth. And look who is here".

She moves and behind her are all my dogs that had passed sitting in a line; they all had a message for me,

Pepi said: "yesterday while they introduced themselves, they told me to tell you thank you and how happy and grateful they are to have been in your life.

"Mom they are all poodles, I told you I'm coming back in a small body so I can go with you everywhere but I think I'm going to come back in a poodle body, you really love poodles mom". Here are the messages.

Charlie, your very first poodle, he said, he knew he needed to come to you trained, so your mom will let you finally keep a dog, that's why he was destructive at your brother's house, he knew he needed to be with you. His mission was to keep your heart open. He got old and feels like he did not completed his mission because there was too much darkness in that house, He said, the day he got euthanized he would have love you hold him in your arms but he knows how difficult it was for you to know that grandma had made the call and the Vet had come to euthanize him, he's grateful that you hold him in your arms all the way to the shooting camp where you finally put his body to rest. He said he loves you extremely and he's guiding Fergie that's why you always had such a strong connection with Fergie.

Daisy: well Daisy poo said her mission was not with you, was not to be your dog, her mission was to open your mother's heart and be her dog, that's why she was never attached to you and never nice to you. She feels she failed her mission because her body got old, she went blind and grandma put her down. She fought the chemical because it was not her time. She had not yet accomplished her mission that's why the Vet had to give her four doses of chemical to euthanized her and the last one in her heart. She's sorry that you had to be there and see it all, because she knows how much you cared for her even though she was always mean to you.

Chiquito: well Chiquito is sorry mom, he's sorry he got out that Sunday morning, he was young and decided to go around the house instead of coming back to the garage door when grandpa called him, he was expecting someone to open the front door but on his way there he got taken and was never able to come back to you. He said: I tried my best to escape from the people that took me but they never let me go. Mom you were right I was taken by the construction workers building the hotel next door to our house. I'm sorry mom now I'm in heaven with Charlie and Daisy and all the others that had live with you after us, I know how hard it was for you to never find me, I know how hard you looked for me, but I've been told you needed to learn a lesson to cope with loss and learn to let go. Mom I love you and I'm sorry.

Collin: well mom you know I'm an experience mommy from all those years at the mill, and I can tell you Collin was just to small when they sold him to you, and Collin said he was missing his mom a lot, and he could not cope with it, he was still too young to go live with a family, he knew how loving you could be to dogs. But he felt he better be with his real mommy and daddy at his birth house, he can't believe the veterinarian had convinced you to buy him and had convinced her parents family to sell him, the Vet knew he was too young, and when his tail got docked he could not bare with more loss and decided to go, yes, he was in pain and he knew you did your best to comfort him, you did your best to save his life, took him to the veterinarian, gave him medication for his tail infection but he was broken hearted from not having his mom so one day he just decided to go and he stopped his heart, he said not to blame the vet, he did what he could even to bring him back but Collin rather be in heaven, he also said he's thankful you take him to rest to your pet burial place with Charlie and Daisy and he's more happy in heaven, he got to always be a puppy mom. To tell you the truth he's too funny and goofy.

Simba: well mom Simba, enjoyed life with you, he said he used to nip your bum when you came from school just to get you out of the serious mind set and he's showing me how he accomplished that many times, how he made you smile and it was a game. You knew you would be nipped at the bum as soon as you got home every day. He said he did enjoy stealing the candy canes at Christmas time and the chocolates, his favorite part was putting the chocolate wrapping back in the chocolate tray at the coffee table and see your mom go crazy blaming you and your dad from eating the chocolates and leaving the garbage behind. He had quite a sense of humor mom; he was and still is a joker. He said he wishes he would not trust people in the house because he got taken by your half-brother who drove him and threw him from the truck into the side of the road, there was a park around so he got his sore body to the park and a homeless guy helped him, then the lady that reported him back to you took him from the homeless guy. He said he's thankful you gave him an ID tag; well he said he knew you learned that lesson with the loss of Chiquito who did not have a tag, but the ID tag brought him back to you. He recovered and was happy with you guys until your half-brother took him again, this time he made sure you never found him, he took him to his ranch and feed him alive to the rottweilers in the ranch, he said not to blame your half-brother, he has forgiven him, and you have to understand your half-brother was entangled in a lot of darkness and a lot of pain, pain of not being loved by his mother and that's why he did what he did. He said he loves you and he's happy in heaven with the rest of us.

Gabriela Duran

With my sissy and my mom, resting in the couch Fall 2010

Now mom I want to show you all these other dogs in the line behind, there is dolly, guerita, la negra, luna, the poodle with the broken leg, the black lab mix you picked up hit by a car and many more they all say thank you, they all know they were not supposed to live with you forever, but they are grateful you took them from the streets or their abusive homes, gave them basic medical care and found them homes. Dolly wants to say she lived four years after you rescued her in a ranch where she ran happy and free under the sky, thank you for taking her out of that garage and gave her vaccinations and spayed her, that help her find a home.

Guerita said, she escaped from her house that you found her but she lived happy rooming the streets of Monterrey without worrying of having more puppies. La negra is happy that you picked her up from Walmart parking lot where she was dropped off and took her to Prodan, grateful that you found her a home. Broken leg poodle, well he knew his leg was beyond repair, and he knew he had to hide from people to survive, so he's grateful you teamed up with that couple on that Saturday caught him and took him to the vet, he knows how difficult was for you to euthanize him but he knows it was the best, and like this guy mom, there are many more you help, and they say you help them even though you had your own pain and darkness going on, you put everything aside and chose love to help them.

Mom I know you don't believe in euthanasia because you think only God has the power to decide over lives. But for all the euthanasia's you had taken the decision to do in life had been an act of love so please don't feel guilty, I know you feel terrible because you took me in, in the morning instead of evening and you had to take the decision yourself, dad wanted to keep me until the evening but you could no longer hear me scream knowing there was nothing else to do, knowing the pain killer did not help me, mommy you did the right thing and I'm grateful for that I love you and as I told you the room was full of angels, all the angels you called in for me, and Fergie my sister was holding the space, she knew I was leaving and I'm grateful you let her come to be with me until the last minute.

Peachy how is heaven?

Mommy heaven is the best, I can run up and down the clouds I have many friends here, animal friends that had the pleasure to live with you or at least know you and human friends too. You know the people from the retirement home that I used to visit, they are here too mom and they love me. I have a huge cloud of my own, so please always look at clouds you will feel me and perhaps see me.

"Mom I want to show you something else", and she steps backs and shows me little apricot poodle baby's, oh Peachy. "Mom these are my babies, the ones I could not keep alive at the puppy mill because I was lacking food and care for them, remember I told you yesterday I did my best and I could not save them, just like you did, just like you tried everything to save me, well here they are and now I have the opportunity to be with them and teach them, I told them about you and told them I'm coming back to live with you. Mom can I take my babies with me?" Oh Peachy you are always welcome, you can bring whoever you want with you my little Angel.

Thanks mom, I promise I'm coming back, you will recognize me by my eyes, I still don't know yet where and when are we meeting again, but I'll let you know and I promise as soon as I see you, I won't let you pass by, I will growl, tau, do all my tricks so you know it is me and you can pick me up and take me.

Me: Thank you my Angel I'll be waiting for you.

Peachy: but mom I'm with you, I'm in heaven but I'm also in the new house, I run up and down the stairs, spend time in the kitchen, go to the dining room table, bark at the door, you know me, I'm also sleeping in bed with you, dada and Fergie. I'm still very present can't you feel me.

Me: yes Peachy I can feel you and I can see you in my mind wagging your tail and running in the house all happy, being the happy girl you were here with us. I also see you a lot in the TV room.

Peachy: mom I know winter is coming and I know you and dada will spend more time in the house so that's why I choose the TV room to spend my last weeks, you will always have me present there.

Me: yes sweetheart but it still hurts lots, the house feels so empty without you and so cold and big.

Peachy: Mom I'm still there so just close your eyes and you will see me running happy and look. (And she smiles and shows me she has all her teeth).

Me: I'm happy you got your teeth back baby girl.

Are you cold in heaven?

Peachy: Mom heaven is like living in Florida, but Friday when I was leaving, I ask the angels if I could take some things with me and they let me, so picture this, while in the Vet clinic, me laying in your arms in my lifeless body. Well I was really in front of you, an angel was holding me in his arms and I had my long hair. I took my pink vest and my crown barrette. I'm looking at you holding me in sadness, Fergie saying her good byes, dad asking to hold me and I don't get it, because I'm happy and healthy in the angels arms, of course they gave me wings immediately, but you know, you have to learn how to use this things so, I chose to be carried to heaven. It was angel Gabriel, who carried me, and Michael, Rafael, Uriel, Chamuel and many others were my escort, it was a super ride mom. I also took my Canada pooch jacket and my snow suite that grand ma made me in case heaven was cold; you know I never liked the cold weather. Or been to hot either. People here say I'm funny wearing my crown barrette everywhere and my pink vest, but I don't care if they laugh. And she smiles.

Me: Peachy you are a princess.

Peachy: smiles

Me: What do you want me to do with all your clothes and stuff?

Peachy: Mom keep them please, can you keep them for 2 years, I'm coming back and I would like to wear all my dresses and barrettes again.

Me: no problem sweet heart, everything will be waiting for you.

Peachy: Mom I want you to understand that I will come back to pick up Andrew, I never like him but he's next coming to heaven and I'll be there, it may be at the end of this year. That's why God send Tyra. Tyra does not supposed to live a long time with you, she is just there to keep Fergie company and help her, once I take Andrew so my sister Fergie doesn't feel depress. After that Tyra may go next and I will come back to be with you and Fergie. Remember you will recognize me because of my eyes.

Me: yes sweetie, my pippin little angel, I love you.

Peachy: Mom I want you to tell dada he doesn't have to be sad when he prepares food dishes. I'm right there with him in the kitchen; tell him to feel me, running around, doing my shark dance, wagging my tail, barking and growling so he hurries with my dish.

Me: I will chiquiletin, dada knows you are here, he can feel you in the kitchen while preparing meals, but I'll remind him.

Peachy: well mom remember I'm here, but I have to go now, also you need to do the dog sausages, they were delicious and very nutritious, you can call them Peachy's choice and it can be part of my foundation, please mom, finish the book and establish my foundation so more people can learn about puppy mills and more lives get save. You know I'm a heart opener, I even open the heart of grandma who doesn't like dogs, you see she even cried yesterday when you told her I had transcended, I believe

I can open the hearts of many more humans with my book and thru my foundation help stop puppy mills for once and for all.

Mom: Yes princess I'm working on it, I promise you, we'll publish your story and we will create a foundation I don't know how but when there is a will there is a way and with your guidance we'll be able to do it.

Mom: love you princess, thank you for staying here and visit me and for all the messages you have sent me thru people too.

Peachy: love you mom, I'll always be with you in spirit and I'll find my way back in a new body so we can have more adventures together. LOL.

For many of you this might be hard to believe, but for me it felt real, and today we can still feel her around the house.

You never know where you will find that soul that will change your life forever. Remember to keep your mind and heart open as this could happen anytime.

How I want the world to remember me.

National Mill dog Rescue

Well through the many pages of this book I have being asking you to keep your minds and hearts open because this book is truly a non-conventional story. But I feel I need to include the story of a woman who I just learned about through her organization's Facebook page. A few months before Peachy's passing, I saw a Facebook posting about National Mill dog Rescue (NMDR). Now, if you look at my Facebook page, you will notice is full of rescue groups, pretty much everything I "like" on my page is either dog rescue related or spirituality related. Having said so, one day this past summer while looking at my Facebook page I saw a posting from NMDR and I got super exited.

Could it be possible that there was someone out there doing what I have dreamed of doing since Peachy came to our lives? Someone fighting puppy mills and trying to exterminate them? Someone saving all this wonderful puppy mill survivors and raising awareness about puppy mills? I went to their website and to my surprise the engine behind this organization is a powerful and amazing woman, Theresa Strader, now one of my heroes.

I have not had the honor to meet Theresa yet, nor do I know if I'll be able to meet her one day, but what this woman is doing for these wonderful puppy mill survivors is truly amazing, and it just totally matches what I, deep in my heart, had being wanting to do all my life. Due to personal experiences, I was a little lost for many years about what direction I should take, but life gave me Peachy so I could get clear on my mission in this lifetime.

And life keeps giving me signs, once I decided I was going to publish Peachy's story to raise awareness and I wanted to support organizations that are dedicated to rescue puppy mill dogs and end puppy mills across the world. There it was. Life put NMDR and their founder right in from of me, just to prove to me that we can do whatever we put our hearts and minds into.

Gabriela Duran

So enough said - here is the story. Theresa started NMDR after going to a dog auction in 2007 and rescuing a dog she found there. Lily was a 7 year old Italian Greyhound who had lived her whole life in a puppy mill. In fact she was a puppy mill mama. As a result Lily had very little bone left in her jaws and had a severely deformed face. Theresa saw beyond Lilly's appearance at that auction and made a promise she was going to take her out of there. Little did she know then that Lily would change her life forever.

Theresa was experienced in rescue but she had never seeing a puppy mill dog before. Sadly Lilly passed away 15 months after Theresa rescued and adopted her. Theresa founded NMDR in February of 2007 with the mission to rescue, rehabilitate, and rehome discarded commercial breeding dogs. At first the rescue was located in her back yard but due to the necessity of housing more puppy mill survivors, Theresa moved the organization to a nearby kennel facility. As of today she and her group of volunteers have rescued more than 8,000 thousands puppy mill survivors. The mission can be challenging due to the conditions these dogs arrive in when they finally reach freedom. In my eyes, this group is unstoppable.

Theresa Strader is also one of the biggest engines behind the cause of educating the public about the cruel realities of the puppy mill industry. She has truly committed her life to rescuing dogs from puppy mills and educating the public about this hidden industry. If you go to NMDR's website or Facebook page you will find many videos of Theresa's work. I highly recommend taking the time to watch some of the videos.

The work this remarkable woman does is titanic; especially because as a rescuer myself I know how hard it can be to raise the funding needed to save lives, so I'm truly amazed by her. I wish one day to have to opportunity to meet her and be part of one of the puppy mill rescue runs into the Midwest.

But in the meantime I want to ask you to please check out their website www.milldogrescue.org, and this holiday season if you are planning on getting a dog, please consider one of the wonderful puppy mill survivors that live at NMDR. I promise you they will change your life forever.

If you are not planning on getting a pet, maybe you would like to make a donation to honor one of your loved ones or a loving pet in heaven? Perhaps Peachy's story will inspire you to donate in her name to keep her memory alive.

I also want to invite you to read Theresa's letter to Lily's breeder. I promise it will change your life forever and maybe inspire you to donate in Lily's memory to keep this rescue going.

So open your heart and help us keep this and many other rescues able to pursue their missions – speaking for those who have no voice.

The way I see it, there are many ways to help, you don't have to go and open your own shelter, maybe you can just spread the word about a wonderful rescue organization, or any rescue group that you love. Or maybe you cans save your spare change and donate it to a rescue; or spend some of your time at the local shelter walking dogs? You can do it in loving memory of one of your loved ones; I promise this will make your heart sing.

I'm more hands on and even though I'm planning to make a donation with the profits of Peachy's book, I'm also planning on go to Colorado and hoping to be able to help NMDR on one of their rescue rides, who knows, perhaps my dog groomer skills can be of help to them.

So what I'm saying is open your heart and get involved; see beyond and help another soul in need, just like Theresa and many other wonderful rescuers do.

We are all souls having an earth experience and it feels great to help.

Have faith; listen to your soul and Believe.

Afterword

I hope you enjoyed this story. Even though writing a book to raise awareness about dogs and promote adoption, had been in the back of my mind for over 10 years, sharing our life with Peachy only made it clear that I needed to do it.

I'm thankful for the seven wonderful years of teachings Peachy shared with us, having her only made us more humans and more connected to our souls.

We for sure wish Peachy would have lived long enough to see this book and to see her life suffering was not in vain. Perhaps she could have done book signings, I'm sure she would have loved that.

I hope you help us by recommending this book to your friends and family. I really was as honest during my writing as I could have been, after all I'm human and I'm imperfect so I did make a few mistakes over the years, maybe it was part of my learning and maybe, if I ever get to share my life with another puppy mill survivor I will know better.

I'm not saying having a puppy mill survivor as a family pet is hard, because it really wasn't, but I did take many things for granted, having been an experience rescuer, I though at the beginning Peachy just needed time to heal, time to adapt to her new life, and in reality she needed more than just time, she needed spiritual guidance and help that she got thru the animal communicators and healers that help her in her journey on earth as a pet. It took me a year to realize she needed this and maybe if I would have enrolled her with an animal communicator since day one, she would have not have the seizures for example, yes I do have regrets, my biggest one is not knowing if I did enough for her.

Again I'm not saying every single puppy mill survivor needs spiritual guidance, many of them just adapt fast and easily to their new life as a pet, but for my little Peachy spiritual guidance was needed. Perhaps because she was so tiny she really felt helpless at the puppy mill, and she allowed herself to feel unworthy of love. Or perhaps as she once said "I'm very sensitive".

I like to think of her as a very sensitive little kid that the minimal punishment would leave a scar on their life forever. Well Peachy did live five years in punishment (at the puppy mill) and two years as a rescued dog with no hope of getting her own family, every potential adopter, rejected her as soon as they learned she would not trust humans. Don't that would make you feel unworthy? I know that would have made me feel like life is not worth living. What is life without love, truly? And that's pretty much were Peachy was at when I met her.

Peachy changed our life for the better, my husband, myself and my Fergie decided to devote our life to teach and give this little princess warrior all she needed to thrive, to feel worthy again, and now that she is no longer with us, her teachings keep us going.

For Fergie, Peachy was truly like having the puppy she never had, even though Peachy was far away from puppyhood. And for us seeing how Fergie could evolve to be a loving sister-teacher, how she was able to leave her status of princess dog and step down to teach this shattered little survivor, how Fergie was by Peachy's side all the way until the last moment, and how Peachy looked all the time for Fergie was truly the most beautiful thing I have ever live thru.

The sisterhood these two girls' shared, the love and respect they had for each other, even though they were born a month apart and they came from very different walks of life, they decided to be sisters as soon as they met.

I can only imagine how different Peachy' life would had been if she would have come into my life as soon as she was born, I can tell you one thing for sure, she would have been a spoiled rotten princess and she would not have that innocence she had all the time. Peachy was truly an innocent, gentle soul, she was an Angel on earth.

I now see Fergie as a very kind soul and I will always respect her for all the things she did for Peachy. Don't get me wrong she has always been loved and respected but now she is in a different level of love and respect. Fergie before Peachy was used to be the center of attention, the pretty show dog, and the only female in the house, life revolved around her, even though she shared the house with other dogs. She could have easily gone into jealousy and ego, try to beat Peachy down, try to teach her who was number one, but instead she chose love and decided to help her. This for me is only confirmation that animals do communicate in between each other.

It was like Fergie knew from day one Peachy needed to be helped, and to be taken under her wings. Fergie once refer to Peachy as "my student"; I think Fergie had it write Peachy sure was her student. Fergie was Peachy's strength and safety, no matter what experience Peachy was going thru Fergie was there for her, and that's probably what made Peachy trips and new experiences so much easier for her.

I remember people used to always ask us if Peachy was Fergie's baby when we were out for walks. Peachy was a lighter shade of apricot and because her small size people often thought she was a puppy while on walks. They were always surprise to learn Peachy was a puppy mill survivor, that she was the same age as Fergie and that she came to live with us when she was already seven years old. I guess the bond these two had look to people as motherhood.

Fergie is missing Peachy; we know that, even though Peachy was not walking for the last month of her life, so she really was not following Fergie everywhere. Fergie knew of Peachy's condition and visited her all the time, jumped with her in Peachy's bed, and tried her best to keep her company.

I have always loved Fergie but after seeing her go such lengths to keep her "sister" safe and comfortable I have a deeper respect for her.

We sure hope to enjoy Fergie for many years more, perhaps if she feels like it we will get her another puppy mill survivor she can teach, but only if she wants to do so.

For Ricardo and me, losing Peachy was like losing a daughter, because after all she was our first baby together. We had Fergie and Andrew before her but they were my dogs or as I call them my kids, Peachy was our first "kid" together.

Fergie and Peachy biggest lesson to us is "Be kind, step out of your way to help a soul in need, you never know but you may gain a sister".

And with that I leave you, I'm sure I will still receive many lessons from Fergie and from Peachy when she decides to visit me again in my dreams or during meditation.

Love to you.
Gabriela

Abbreviations

AKC American Kennel Club
CKC Canadian Kennel Club
FCM Federacion Canofila Mexicana
FCI Federacion Canofila Internacional
AC Air Conditioner
Vet Veterinarian
MVS Michigan Veterinary Specialist
NMDR National Mill Dog Rescue

Glossary

Comercial Breeding Facility or Puppy mill. Place where people holds hundreds of dogs in small crates. Of course every dog will have their own crate but these crates are not big enough for the dogs to walk or move around. The favorite type of crate among puppy millers is the wire one, with wire floors, because it allows the "breeder/puppy miller" to stack the cages, also allows the waste from the dogs to fall down thru the bottom of the cages until it reaches de floor.

The dogs living in his cages never get out of them; they are often kept in the dark with minimal food and water. These dogs live in filthy environments and are barely alive have no other propose but to produce puppies that latter are sold at pet stores or online thru a broker.

For the puppy miller these dogs are livestock, if the dogs injure themselves the puppy miller will not provide medical attention, these dogs have no names, and they will most times have an ID tag pierced in one of the ears.

Puppy mills are true hells on earth and many dog souls are suffering day after day just because we still purchase puppies instead of making adoption our first choice.

Exercise:

Close your eyes and think of yourself locked in a 2 meter by two meter room or a half bathroom size of room, you can't get out, someone brings you food when they feel like it and will put the food thru the bottom part of the door. You can't go anywhere, water is limited so you don't need to pee, it gets really hot in the summers and really cold in the winters and you have nothings to comfort yourself with, year after year past and the only human contact you have abuses you all the time.

Now ask yourself, how does my soul feels?, how do I feel?
Well the dogs that are lock at the puppy mill producing puppies don't feel any different than you would in their situation.
Something to really reflect on!.

About the Author

Gabriela Duran was born in Mexico. Being an only child of her father second marriage, she grew up surrounded by adults, and pets, lots of different animals.

Her father an animal lover himself, took Gabriela every single weekend of her early years to ranches, so Gabriela had the opportunity to enjoy the outdoors, ride horses, see and feed other farm animals and even being attacked by a turkey at age three.

The turkey kicks her on her back and she went face down to the floor while at the ranch, that was her first turkey pet. The owner of the ranch gave it to her parents to of course kill it and eat it. But Gabriela had a different idea, once the turkey made it to the house she wanted to keep it as a pet, this of course did not happen, Gabriela's mom killed the turkey later that same week and cooked it.

Gabriela also had other pets, like parrots, canaries, a bunny rabbit, fish, turtles, a cat (that she got from the streets), chickens and of course dogs. When she was born they were a couple of working dogs already in the house that belonged to her father and her older half-brother.

Gabriela has never been afraid of dogs but instead, she has always had a deep connection with them. She got her first dog at age three; a brown cocker spaniel that did not last her long, due to her mother not being an animal lover, the dog disappeared.

At age four Gabriela got to keep a short hair German pointer that was born in the house but he died of parvovirus, and soon when she turned six her late half-brother Jorge gave Gabriela the first dog she got to keep, a red toy poodle named Charlie. Charlie lived several years and Gabriela grew a deep love for dogs especially poodles, later in life living in Mexico, she started to be aware of the stray dogs running around and the misery they live thru.

She decided she needed to do something about it, this was not easy since her mother practically hates animals, so Gabriela was not allowed to bring strays home. When she turned seventeen, she got involved with the local kennel club and met more people like her, crazy dog lovers, soon she realized she was not the only one wanting to change the life of unwanted animals; there was a sense of belonging somewhere and just feel very comfortable with the people around her, people that where completely different to what she had met before.

People from all walks of life, and later in life during her University years, she got the opportunity to move to a bigger city where she joined a rescue group, this was back in 2001 and since then she kept the idea she needed to do something bigger to help dogs in need, but what?, how? And in México?.

She was also in to the world of dog Shows, since at age eighteen she got very involved into dog shows, and dog obedience training. It was her way of escaping the real chaotic world she felt trapped in and sees a world of love, companionship and friendship.

As of today Gabriela keeps helping dogs in need, now living in Canada with her three poodles; She has found a way to rescue and bring to good Canadian homes Mexican dogs in need, but still wants to do more for the dogs of the world.

She truly believes helping ending the suffering of unwanted dogs is what she was put in this world for, and this book is the beginning of this mission or at least is how she sees it, Peachy was finally the first rescue dog that Gabriela is being able to keep and well Peachy was also a teacher.

With my entire heart I hope you enjoy this story and together we can make the difference for unwanted dogs.

"Be the change you want to see in the world".

CPSIA information can be obtained at www.ICGtesting.com
Printed in the USA
LVOW08s0302120214

373285LV00001B/65/P